Praise for *Go Back and Get It*

"A fascinating American odyssey quite unlike any other you are likely to encounter, beautifully written, heartfelt, at times painfully candid, and deeply moving."

—Joyce Carol Oates

"*Go Back and Get It* tells the remarkable story of Dionne Ford's search for healing both in the present and in the past. This book offers inspiration and hope for everyone who wants to discover their ancestry and who seeks to connect their own trauma to larger social structures. Ford's thesis that America is founded on the rape of black women is convincing and terrible, but her understanding is a gift and a triumph."

—Alice Elliott Dark, author of
Fellowship Point and *In the Gloaming*

"Few writers offer both urgent clarity of vision *and* arresting, innovative, powerful prose, but Ford does with *Go Back and Get It*. The stakes of this book could not be higher—what Ford is writing for here is nothing less than to save her own life and the lives of other Black and multiracial women—but line by line, this book is perfect."

—Emma Copley Eisenberg,
author of *The Third Rainbow Girl*

"*Go Back and Get It* nails that magical balance only the best memoirs can manage, equal parts unflinching and tender. With effortless prose, Ford shares a captivating story that teaches us not only about her life, but about ourselves—as individuals and as a nation—and positions her as an essential American literary voice."

—Sara Nović, author of *True Biz*

"In this piercing, moving memoir, Ford opens the doors to her family's past and reclaims the lost history of her enslaved ancestors, finding healing for her personal traumas and offering a vision of how our nation might heal its own. She shows us that the painful truths we often keep buried are the ones we must unearth if we are ever to become whole."

—Rachel L. Swarns,
author of *American Tapestry* and *The 272*

"Ford's tenacious, openhearted, poetic *Go Back and Get It* took my breath away. On her thirty-eighth birthday, Ford found a photo of her great-great-grandmother with the white man who'd enslaved her—also Ford's ancestor—and two of the six children they had together. Seeing these forerunners of her own most wrenching experiences deepened and clarified a search that Ford had been moving toward since childhood. The result is transcendent: memoir and quest, critique and exhortation, a distillation of wisdom profound as the Psalms."

—Maud Newton, author of *Ancestor Trouble*

GO BACK
AND GET IT

GO BACK AND GET IT

A Memoir of Race,
Inheritance,
and
Intergenerational Healing

DIONNE FORD

BOLD TYPE BOOKS

New York

Bold Type Books
30 Irving Place, 10th Floor New York, NY 10003
www.boldtypebooks.org
@BoldTypeBooks

Printed in the United States of America

First Edition: April 2023

Published by Bold Type Books, an imprint of Perseus Books, LLC, a subsidiary of Hachette Book Group, Inc. Bold Type Books is a co-publishing venture of the Type Media Center and Perseus Books.

The Hachette Speakers Bureau provides a wide range of authors for speaking events. To find out more, go to hachettespeakersbureau.com or email HachetteSpeakers@hbgusa.com.

Bold Type books may be purchased in bulk for business, educational, or promotional use. For more information, please contact your local bookseller or the Hachette Book Group Special Markets Department at special.markets@hbgusa.com.

The publisher is not responsible for websites (or their content) that are not owned by the publisher.

Print book interior design by Jeff Williams

Library of Congress Cataloging-in-Publication Data
Names: Ford, Dionne, 1969– author.
Title: Go back and get it : a memoir of race, inheritance, and intergenerational healing / Dionne Ford.
Description: First edition. | New York : Bold Type Books, 2023.
Identifiers: LCCN 2022030082 | ISBN 9781645030133 (hardcover) | ISBN 9781645030157 (ebook)
Subjects: LCSH: Ford, Dionne, 1969– | African American women Authors—Biography. | Generational trauma—United States. | African Americans—Social conditions. | Race discrimination—United States—History. | United States—Race relations.
Classification: LCC E185 .F594 2023 | DDC 305.896/0730092 [B]—dc23/eng/20221206
LC record available at https://lccn.loc.gov/2022030082

ISBNs: 9781645030133 (hardcover), 9781645030157 (ebook)

LSC-C

Printing 1, 2023

For my grandmothers and the three Ds—
thank you for finding me.

Glory be to the girl who goes back for her body.

—DOMINIQUE CHRISTINA, *Star Gazer*

CONTENTS

Contents

*From left to right: Unnamed girl,
my great-great-grandfather Colonel W. R. Stuart,
my great-great grandmother Tempy Burton,
Elizabeth McCauley Stuart, unnamed girl.*

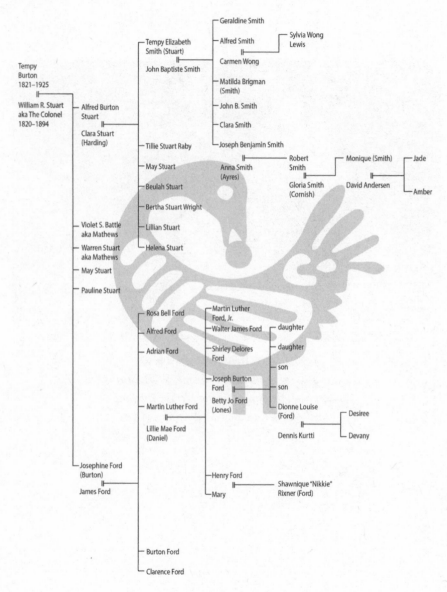

Tempy Burton 1821–1925

William R. Stuart aka The Colonel 1820–1894

— Alfred Burton Stuart
Clara Stuart (Harding)

— Tempy Elizabeth Smith (Stuart)
John Baptiste Smith

— Geraldine Smith
— Alfred Smith
Carmen Wong
— Matilda Brigman (Smith)
— John B. Smith
— Clara Smith
— Joseph Benjamin Smith
Anna Smith (Ayres)

— Sylvia Wong Lewis

— Robert Smith
Gloria Smith (Cornish)

— Monique (Smith)
David Andersen

— Jade
— Amber

— Tillie Stuart Raby
— May Stuart
— Beulah Stuart
— Bertha Stuart Wright
— Lillian Stuart
— Helena Stuart

— Violet S. Battle aka Mathews
— Warren Stuart aka Mathews
— May Stuart
— Pauline Stuart

— Josephine Ford (Burton)
James Ford

— Rosa Bell Ford
— Alfred Ford
— Adrian Ford

— Martin Luther Ford
Lillie Mae Ford (Daniel)

— Martin Luther Ford, Jr.
— Walter James Ford
— Shirley Delores Ford
— Joseph Burton Ford
Betty Jo Ford (Jones)

— daughter
— daughter
— son
— son
— Dionne Louise (Ford)
Dennis Kurtti

— Desiree
— Devany

— Henry Ford
Mary

— Shawnique "Nikkie" Rixner (Ford)

— Burton Ford
— Clarence Ford

Tempy's Family Tree

AUTHOR'S NOTE

IN ORDER TO WRITE THIS BOOK, I RELIED ON MY PERSONAL journals, memory, the memory of others, and research. There are no composed or composite characters in this book, but I did sometimes change or omit names and places to protect privacy.

PROLOGUE
A RELATION

If you are going to look for your enslaved ancestors, you will have to look for the people who enslaved them. Any African American can expect that 19 percent of their ancestors were White men.[1] So, the enslavers might also be your relatives. This is a study in contrasts. Shadow. Light. Black. White. Joy. Pain. Victim. Perpetrator. You will find ephemera—editorials, photographs, wedding announcements—and atrocities—lynched uncles, your people as property in someone's will, deed, or mortgage guarantee. You will also find the living—third cousins once removed, fifth cousins straight up, and descendants of the family that forced your family into slavery. You will meet them on beaches, in dusty archives, in farmhouses, scratching at the past like it is a lotto game and you are strokes away from a million more reasons to believe. For a time, you will cease to believe in or pray to God and instead will pray to your ancestors, the enslaved ones, the women, because they are what you want to be: Mother. Creator. Feminine. Divine. They were raped. They were sold away. They kept on living. Some even thrived. If you are going to look for your enslaved ancestors, you will have to reconsider the word "lucky."

In 1858, when Colonel W. R. Stuart, a wealthy Louisiana cotton broker, married Elizabeth McCauley, a girl from a long line of North Carolina plantation owners, her family gave the couple a slave named Tempy Burton as a wedding gift. Elizabeth was sickly and couldn't have children, but Tempy could and did have six of them with her new master, the Colonel. My great-grandmother, Josephine, born a decade after slavery ended, was their youngest child.

On my thirty-eighth birthday, I found their picture on the internet.

It was May 7, 2007, and with those sevens I'd like to tell you that I was feeling lucky. Tempy was in the middle of the photo. Her former masters, Elizabeth and the Colonel, were sitting behind her. On either side of Tempy were two biracial-looking girls. The one on the left was curly haired and creamy skinned, like my dad and my daughters. It was eerie how this century-old photo of my ancestors mirrored the new family I'd created.

Lucky and unlucky number seven.

In seven days, God made the world. In seven plagues God could wipe it out. On the seventh of May, I was born. In my seventh year, I was raped. It's been said that it takes seven years for every cell in your body to change. In the seven years after finding the family photo, I crisscrossed the country, uncovering the stories of the people in it, and a breach began to mend in me. There is a name for this kind of pilgrimage. The Akan of western Africa call it sankofa. Symbolized by a bird in flight with its head craned backward and an egg in its beak, "sankofa" means to go back and get it, or "it is not wrong to go back for that which you have forgotten."[2]

CHAPTER 1

BLACK ON THE INSIDE

Two years before I found the photo of my ancestors, I couldn't feel my skin. I knew I was there in the shower, but slightly removed, hovering just above myself like a tilde. "Wake up." I yelled, slapped, and pinched myself, but I felt nothing, not the heat of the water nor the slippery porcelain under my feet.

My therapist called it a dissociative episode.

Dissociation: the disconnection or separation of something from something else or the state of being disconnected. Relation: from the Latin, to carry back, the act of telling or recounting. The person who abused me.

Any host of things could have triggered it. My brother's deployment the day before to Iraq, raising two girls whose ages combined equaled mine when I was molested, writing about my abuse for the first time. How would I raise my daughters with confidence and teach them to take care of themselves when I couldn't keep my mind from splintering, when I couldn't clearly define their enemies? I taught them to beware of stranger danger, but my danger, my betrayer, was in my family. Then there is the ultimate betrayal, of ourselves and our own bodies.

We were snuggled into the crease of my daughter's sleigh bed, reading *Black Is Brown Is Tan*, about an interracial family made up of the same parts as ours. The sun dripped in through the slanted wooden shades and made shadows on the peach walls in her bedroom.

"You look just like the girl in the book." I pointed to the curly hair and brown eyes. The girl's skin was darker than my five-year-old's.

"I don't look like her, Mommy. She's Black," my daughter said.

"Well, she's part Black and so are you."

"No, I'm not. I'm White. Just look at me." She held out her arms as proof. Butterscotch skin, thick copper curls. It was easy to see that White was only half the story. Her father, Dennis, is White, with his Irish grandmother's freckled skin and red hair and his Finnish grandfather's long limbs and blue eyes. I am Black, cocoa colored like my grandmothers from Oklahoma and Mississippi.

The horror I felt must have registered on my face because she smiled and added, "I know I'm Black on the inside 'cause I was in your belly, Mommy."

That seemed much worse, like an inverted Oreo. Kids at school always called me "Oreo" because of how I talked, the Duran Duran albums I listened to, the etymology classes I got excited about, all proof to them of White insides.

This wasn't supposed to happen.

My husband and I moved across the river from Manhattan to Montclair, New Jersey, when Desiree was an infant because, according to *Interrace Magazine,* this suburb twelve miles west of the city was the best place for interracial families to live. The kids in my daughter's preschool were different colors, from different cultures and classes. Every day I happily sent her off to its cocoon of otherness.

Then, on our way to preschool one morning, Desiree asked why I call myself Black when—she pointed—I wasn't black like the SUV idling in the drop-off.

"That's just how people of our race, of my race, have described themselves, or have been called by other people . . ." I stammered before she lost interest and started singing along with a *Music for Aardvarks* CD.

What had kept me clinging to "Black"? Even when people began to follow Jesse Jackson's lead in adopting "African American," I gripped tightly onto "Black." Africa was a massive and varied continent, and my people had been in America for centuries. African might have been my ancestry but Black was my experience. I wanted to define myself. Desiree did too. For both of us this was tricky business.

I was her age when I told my sister that I wanted to be White so the mixed girl up the road and the Asian girl down it would stop calling my hair nappy and saying my skin looked "like doo-doo." Up to that point, I'd liked my color. And I didn't give much thought to the varieties of skin tone in my family until a few years after that, when my dad picked me up from a cheerleading squad sleepover and the hostess asked if he was "White or something." His father, my grandfather, Martin Luther Ford, had pin-straight black hair and was as White as any White man I'd ever seen. Until I was twelve I never questioned why he looked so different from my brothers and sisters and me, the darkest of us all.

That summer, Grandpa visited us in New Jersey for the first time. It might have even been his first time across the Mason-Dixon Line; we usually visited him at his home in a New Orleans project near the French Quarter. Grandpa was in his late seventies by then, legally blind although he insisted he could see, and he spent most days at the senior center while my parents were at work. In the two hours between when the senior center bus dropped him at the end of our driveway and when my mother came home, it was up to me to entertain him and make sure he didn't burn the house down.

As an almost-teen, I wanted nothing to do with adults, let alone an old man with a slow drawl and bad hearing. Grandpa mostly listened to baseball on the radio and made small talk about the weather. Then one day he came home with a hand-painted macaroni necklace, slipping it over my head as I poured him a glass of iced tea.

"I made a little somethin' for ya, sugah," he said.

I pinched the pasta pieces like I was praying the rosary and asked: "Grandpa, are you White?"

He didn't hesitate. He wasn't White, he said, but he used to pretend he was to get better-paying jobs when New Orleans was segregated. Grandpa had delivered groceries throughout the city without any of his White customers realizing that a Black man was entering through their front doors and handling their food. At night, he took whatever seat he wanted on the trolley car, something his wife and children could never do.

He was more interested in telling me about how he'd passed for White at the grocery store than how he'd come to have such fair skin. And so I found myself at twelve preparing for my life in journalism with reluctant interviewees, rephrasing the same question over and over in hopes of a different response.

"Do you have any White kin?" I tried. "Why are you so White looking?"

"Well, I didn't know my grandfather, but Momma said he was a White man called Stuart," he said. "He owned the plantation that my grandmother worked on."

That was an interesting way of putting it.

I asked Grandpa outright, "Was your grandmother a slave?"

He didn't answer me directly. "My momma said those Stuarts were a fighting bunch, but not with the help, only with each other," he said. "They treated their house people good."

Grandpa had lived in a house on some of Stuart's property, and my dad, with his brothers and sister, had been raised there too. The house was big enough that Grandpa rented out rooms to other families to pay the taxes. But eventually they lost the house, Grandpa said, "because of Stuart's relatives." I imagined a Scarlett O'Hara–style plantation with big hurricane shutters and a long dirt road that stretched to the Gulf of Mexico like a thirsty tongue.

I didn't know what he meant about Stuart's relatives, but I didn't ask anything more. I didn't ask what Josephine, Grandpa's mother, looked like; I didn't ask if he'd ever met his grandmother or knew her name, or if she and Stuart had other children. The next time I saw my grandfather, three years later, I was concerned more about the braces on my teeth and if a boy would ever like me than about my family history. He was in a nursing home and we could all tell as we filed into the antiseptic room that he wasn't long for this world.

If he were still alive, he would surely sit my daughter in his lap, stare down at her from behind his Coke-bottle glasses like she ought to know better, and solve the equation of her identity like it was simple math. He would tell her in his Louisiana drawl, "Look here: I'm Black; my momma, Josephine, was Black; and so are you. It doesn't matter what you look like."

When I was a kid in the seventies, "Black Is Beautiful" was still a battle cry. An afro pick in the back of a pocket, a Black fist clutching the handle, was a sacred symbol. To call yourself even half White, no matter how you looked, was a sacrilege. Touting your Native American ancestry was suspicious too. It implied that being Black was something to be ashamed of. Even pretending was a no-no: my mom gave me a good yelling once for draping a towel over my head, swinging it back and forth, and asking how she thought I'd look with blonde hair and blue eyes. So when Barack Obama described himself as Black and not biracial while on the campaign trail, I understood. He was not from my daughters' generation but mine, a time when "one drop of blood" ruled and one had to choose.

Wasn't choice what I wanted for her? When my daughter told everyone to call her Liam, because she wanted to try on a boy's name, I happily obliged. When she decided to wear open-toed shoes in the winter, I told her to throw on some socks. But the insistence that she was "a little White girl" dug a hole in me. And yet I knew that what I was asking her to do at five, embrace all of herself, was something that, at almost forty, I had never really done myself.

Like Grandpa, I also passed, but in my own way. I hid behind my husband's Whiteness. When we first started to look for places to live together, I often sent him alone out of fear that my Black face would diminish our rental options. I hid behind his maleness and quit my first big-time job at a national news outlet soon after we got married to be a full-time wife. I hoped he would be enough of a person for the two of us. Almost always the only Black person in the room, the apartment building, the office, I made myself palatable so as not to offend or scare anyone.

This kind of passing has its limits. It didn't save me from being confused for my daughter's nanny by a neighbor who had watched my belly grow for nine months and had seen me riding the elevator in our apartment building for a full year. That neighbor was White, but the Black nannies in Central Park thought I was my daughter's babysitter too.

"There are too many Blacks," a young new immigrant from Poland told me when I asked her how she liked the town she'd moved to, not far from ours. We were interviewing her for the job of watching our children. She looked me right in the face when she said it. Then she smiled and told me how cute my kids were. I smiled back at her, because that's what I'd taught myself to do, wear the mask.[1] It's what I do at every family gathering when I sit down to eat with the person who raped me. It's what I'm doing right now in not disclosing his name. In my own country, in my own family, I have been an invisible woman.

I put Desiree's book back on the shelf, tucked her under the covers. Everything was in its place, but the room felt different, transformed into a shotgun-style gateway in which I could see clearly behind and ahead of me. A few months had passed since the dissociative episode, but I was still scared to death that I was going crazy, that I would have to be medicated, that I was damaged goods. The men in my family had gone off to war, but I was the one diagnosed with PTSD. I tried eye movement desensitization and reprocessing therapy. I went to an energy healer, a medium, started going to more twelve-step meetings, started playing capoeira, stopped eating sugar and wheat—anything to keep from going back there. But maybe I needed to go back there.

"To know ourselves as we are," Alice Walker wrote in *In Search of Our Mothers' Gardens*, "we must know our mothers' names."

My acting coach once told our class that to embody a character and bring it to life, "you want to know your lines so well that you can forget them." Once the lines become second nature, he said, we could be free, fully present in the moment and in the scene. I wanted to know my history that way. I wanted it to anchor and root me, my daughters too, bring me to life, bring us back into our bodies.

To get to this true north, I would head south, to New Orleans, my father's hometown. But before I could finish planning the trip, Hurricane Katrina hit. So, instead, my family attended a Katrina victim fund-raiser not far from our house in the Watchung Mountains, where we hiked an easy trail to the overlook that was also a 9/11 memorial. There, at the mountain's edge, the New York City skyline spread out over the American flags lining the memorial wall like a six-year-old's gap-toothed smile. My daughter doesn't remember what used to be there, how we drove to that spot to watch the horror unfold, helpless and afraid. She doesn't know that I still look to those absent icons while navigating some unfamiliar route to orient myself, find my way home. My eye is always drawn to the gap where the Twin Towers used to be, like a tongue to a lost tooth. Empty spaces have shaped me.

My grandfather Martin Luther Ford, seated, with his brother Adrian, c. 1910.

CHAPTER 2

BORROWING HISTORY

Eye movement desensitization reprocessing was supposed to change my neural pathways, so I figured it would involve heavy machinery. I imagined something metal and bulky that would be connected to my fingertips or the top of my head, like in *A Clockwork Orange.*

Trauma alters your brain, pitting it with grooves, my longtime therapist had told me. The earlier in life that you experience trauma, the deeper and trickier the groove. Mine felt like a ditch I kept falling into. EMDR was supposed to fill in the ditch, smooth out the grooves. My therapist had heard good things about this new treatment, but wasn't trained in it, so I'd sought out a practitioner. The EMDR office was in the basement of a building downtown and it looked pretty much like every other therapist's office I'd been to since I'd started therapy at nineteen. There was no heavy machinery, no wiring, in this next phase of my recovery—just my memories, the practitioner, and a pencil.

The EMDR practitioner would tell me to think of a traumatic event and then follow the pencil she was holding with my eyes. That's how we spent the session, not discussing the details of every trauma, the way I did in psychotherapy. I would just bring the event to mind and she would move the pencil while I trailed it with my gaze. We did this with the episode of incest. We did this with my being left alone for hours after a football game in the middle of a cornfield when I was nine, with the murder of my neighbor that same year, with the college rape. We did it with my high school graduation; my abuser was the only person in my family who attended.

The practitioner asked me to rate my discomfort around each recalled incident on a scale from one to ten. Incest? Ten. Abandonment? Ten. Murder? Eight. Rape? Nine. After I followed the pencil, things that had started out at ten dropped down to four or five.

By the end of our session, something had shifted. I felt subtly but sustainably different. It wasn't a new feeling, though. It was old. It was primal. It was the feeling I had when I was little, lying in the grass, staring at the clouds, or twirling a buttercup between my fingers, kneeling in my first church, our yard. It was that feeling—fresh and awake and full of wonder. "A child wakes up over and over again and notices that she's living," Annie Dillard wrote in "To Fashion a Text." I'd woken up so many times there, in the woods that dotted our neighborhood, the honeysuckle bush at the end of our block where I had my first kiss, and now again. I began observing everything for the sake of observing as opposed to surveying and appraising: the clear late-summer sky; the practitioner's hair, which matched her eyes and her affect, flat and dull, but it didn't matter because I was no longer flatlining. No more whiplash, no more bracing, no more clenching, no more driving down a severely potholed road on high alert. EMDR would not inoculate me against new or repeated trauma, but in just a couple of sessions, I could go back there without getting stuck there.

I experienced the ordinariness of myself, the people in my life, my body, and none of it felt under threat (my body) or threatening (the people around me). The heavens didn't part. I wasn't struck with unconditional love for my family. I didn't feel at peace with everyone and everything, but I did feel of a piece. Beginning, middle, end.

Stories are medicine. We tell them to get better. Sometimes, like Scheherazade, we tell them to save our own lives. Trauma disorders memory, fragmenting our stories. As I trailed the pencil, for the first time in a long time, I was integrated.

A FOOT OF SNOW COVERED THE GROUND IN EARLY MAY WHEN my parents brought me home from the hospital. I was born in Maine, the Whitest state in the country, and raised in what abolitionists called the slave state of the North, New

Jersey—the only state in the Union that never voted for Lincoln and the last to abolish slavery.

My parents grew up in Oklahoma and Louisiana. Their parents were from Oklahoma, Arkansas, and Mississippi. I've been to the farm where my maternal grandfather used to grow soy and cotton and to the little house bounded by red clay where my maternal great-grandmother made fresh buttermilk biscuits in a kitchen so clean you could eat off the floor. (Cozied up under her square Formica table, I sometimes did.)

There was a heft to my maternal line, but my father's people and their places were harder to grasp, like river reeds. We visited his birthplace on the Gulf Coast of Mississippi only once, the Easter before I turned seven, as the country was celebrating its bicentennial. It was sandy and piney, like our town in rural South Jersey. Dad never told people he was born in Mississippi, just that he was from New Orleans, where he'd gotten his schooling.

Dad had started high school at Gilbert Academy, a multistory stone structure with towers, turrets, and groomed lawns in the bourgeois part of New Orleans, funded by the Methodist Church. He was instructed in violin, introduced to Black fraternities, and poised to join alumni like Andrew Young, Ellis Marsalis, and Margaret Alexander, author of the poem "For My People" and *Jubilee*, a novel based on the life of her enslaved great-great-grandmother. Then, a year after he enrolled, the academy shut down and the school's four-acre property was sold to the Catholic archdiocese. My father transferred to the McDonogh High School on

Rampart, "a street of hookers, tailors, and pool rooms," he told me.

During Mardi Gras, one of Dad's Black classmates lost an eye when he was beaten on the streets of the French Quarter by several White sailors on leave. Skirmishes with White sailors were common, and my father feared he could be next. He dropped out of high school months shy of graduation to join the recently desegregated Air Force. His mother, Lillie Mae, had to sign a waiver for him to enlist since he was only seventeen. As the train that took him to basic training crossed the Mason-Dixon Line, for the first time in his life he was told by the conductor that he could sit wherever he wanted.

That was in the 1950s, as the Korean War was coming to an end. After basic training, my father was stationed in Ramsgate, England. My grandfather, Alonzo Walton, was stationed there too, with his wife and teenage daughter, who would become my mother. Granddaddy Alonzo had been driving oxen, breaking up the dry Arkansas soil, and picking cotton on his family's farm since he was old enough to tie a basket to his back and strike an ox with a switch—around age six. He joined the military at eighteen "so he didn't have to be a slave anymore," my grandmother once told me, and he remained there for forty-six years. All the while, the couple built businesses: a barbecue, a trailer park with a grocery store, and a few small rental properties in New Jersey. One of those properties abutted a church and had three worn gravestones on the front lawn that belonged to Black soldiers who'd fought for the Union in the Civil War.

We lived a few miles from my mom's parents on a half-paved, half-dirt road on the tip of the Pine Barrens outside of both the Army and the Air Force bases. Dense woods surrounded us on the side and at the back, so that our only immediate neighbor was a neglected house full of men. I was not allowed in that house, or to play with the three boys who lived there, and was told to steer clear of their father. Theirs was the only all-White family on our block. The rest of our neighbors were Black and German, White and Korean, Japanese, Black and Filipino, Puerto Rican, or Black, like us. Our neighborhood was integrated but my family's story was not.

My fifth-grade teacher, Mrs. Sauer, assigned our class the task of drawing the flag of the country our family came from. Old Glory was off limits. We'd all come from somewhere else, she said. When we brought in our homemade flags, signaling our immigrant status, we'd all be the same, on equal footing. That was the idea.

When I asked my dad that night what country in Africa he thought we came from, he let out a heavy, frustrated sigh.

"Between the Indian blood and the slave blood, we've been here longer than anybody. Who's more American than us?" He put his feet up on the coffee table, crossed them with a one-two thud of the ankles. That was that.

I knew about the "Indian" blood: my great-great-grandmother from Oklahoma, on my mom's side. But what about the slave blood? Which of our ancestors had been slaves? Where in Africa had they come from? Dad was sitting under the leopard skin tacked to the paneled family room wall and I was lying on the monkey rug, an enormous circle of sewn-together black and white pelts. My parents had brought the skins back from Ethiopia. They and my siblings had lived there for three years during the reign of Haile Selassie, before I was born. I asked Dad if he thought we could be from Ethiopia, but he said he doubted it. Ethiopia was in the east, and slaves, he said, were brought in from the western coast.

I read my father's emotional temperature: silence plus cocked head meant disappointed and annoyed. My body knew that there was something wrong with my teacher's question. But I couldn't articulate what exactly, or decide how to respond. I didn't have the language. I didn't yet know that this was White supremacy: ask a question that I can't answer because it doesn't include me. Even though my father, my mother's father, and my grandmother's father had all served this country, we still, as author Isabel Wilkerson has put it, "had to act like immigrants in order to be recognized as citizens."[1]

As Dad sliced off squares of Cracker Barrel cheese and popped them into his mouth, I made up our history. I figured that since Dad was from Louisiana and Louisiana had once belonged to France, his fair freckled skin and wavy black curls must be the French blood in him.

When I colored three red, white, and blue stripes on my paper—a sideways, compressed version of Old Glory—it was the first time I betrayed myself for a grade. It was my first act of state-sanctioned self-splitting, and self-abandonment. Trauma expert Dr. Bessel van der Kolk writes in *The Body*

Keeps the Score, "Dissociation means simultaneously knowing and not knowing."

"FOR THE CRAMPED BEWILDERED YEARS WE WENT TO SCHOOL to learn"; my inside story rarely matched the one told about me.[2]

"*The Cosby Show* is like so unbelievable," one of my new friends screamed in the high school cafeteria one day. "How many Black people do you know that don't live in the Hollow?" The Hollow was our suburban equivalent of the projects. We'd moved to northern New Jersey by then so Dad could be closer to his new job in Manhattan. Another friend smiled and gestured at me and the other Black girl at the table, a recent transplant from the Midwest who lived in a mansion in a new, wealthy development.

New friend swiped the air with her hand.

"They don't count," she said. "They're not really Black." She tried to explain that she meant it in a good way, "because you live in a nice house and you're really smart."

What is it about breaking bread that brings out some people's brutality? In South Jersey, at my friend Margaret's dinner table, her father had recognized my last name. He used to report to my dad out on McGuire Air Force Base. Then he or his wife or one of her brothers announced that their dog was trained to sic Black people.

There seemed to be only two ways to be Black, desperately and magically, and my family was neither of these.

Uncle Henry and me in front of the monkey skins,
c. 1975.

CHAPTER 3
BEATING BACK THE FUTURE

At college, I learned things I would have liked to have known as a kid. That race was a social construct, not something biological. That the first laws in the country linked slavery to race and decreed that any child born to a Black woman and fathered by a White man was a slave. That America's economic power was built on the systemic rape of Black women—the original sin of the original sin.

The only Black teachers I'd ever had, before college, were the two women who taught me how to sew and type. Now, two Black women professors were teaching me about American pluralism, minorities in the media, and Black people's contributions to literature. I read slave narratives, I read Malcolm X's autobiography. I was affirmed by *Tar Baby* and *The Color Purple* and regularly advised by a man selling incense and Black Power booklets off Columbus Circle to decolonize my mind and not sleep with the White devil.

"Race is just a thing outside of you," I told my journalism professor in my last semester. "It's a coat of paint."

My professor was interviewing me about my relationship with a White classmate for a national women's magazine. The largest city in the nation had just elected its first Black mayor, Jesse Jackson had visited our university while running for president, and I was in love with a White boy. Meanwhile, New York was imploding. My boyfriend and I had started dating shortly after Yusef Hawkins was killed in Bensonhurst by a group of White men who thought the Black teen was in their neighborhood to visit a White girl. While I was getting my BA in New York: a twenty-three-year-old Black man was killed by a mob of White teens at Howard Beach; five Black and brown boys were wrongfully imprisoned for raping a White woman jogger in Central Park; and six White Saint John's students were deemed innocent of raping their Black classmate. The title of the forthcoming magazine article was "Love vs. Bigotry."

After six months of dating, my boyfriend gave me his claddagh ring. I took a train up to Maine for Memorial Day weekend to meet his parents, but they refused to see me. On the long car ride back, he broke the news that his parents would pull the plug on his college funding if we continued to date. "They're not racist," he said with tears in his eyes. "They're Irish Catholics. They know a thing or two about persecution." I twirled his ring around my finger. Now you see the heart, now you don't.

My professor asked me about the feasibility of interracial relationships in our current climate, and I brought up my great-great-grandparents. "They made it work in Mississippi after the Civil War. I think we can make it work now," I said. I had never told another adult about Tempy and the Colonel before. When she asked me to elaborate, I said that my great-great-grandparents had conceived my great-grandmother, Josephine, raised her in the racist South, and had done just fine. I referred to their relationship as a marriage. My professor looked at me from behind her wavy salt-and-pepper bangs with pity. "They couldn't have been married," she said. "Interracial marriage was against the law."

I'd read *Clotel, Our Nig, Iola Leroy*, and *Incidents in the Life of a Slave Girl* by then, so I must have been familiar with the anti-miscegenation laws that made it illegal for Black and White people to be married. But I had imagined a partnership, my great-great-grandmother whose name I didn't know yet and my great-great-grandfather—White face, splotched red from the heat—surveying an endless field, considering what they'd created. That their alliance was forced, was rape, had never entered my mind.

I'd made every effort not to think about sex and my family. I was nine when an older friend gave me the sex talk in the same matter-of-fact way that I now use to explain uncomfortable things to my daughters. That's when I understood what had happened to me at seven. I prayed to God to forgive me for what my older friend had described as "the big sin." I was a religious child who'd gone to summer Bible camp for fun, and the implications of what I'd done weighed on me daily. I didn't think of it as an act of violence perpetrated against me, but rather as a sin that I had unwittingly committed. I was going to hell. No boy would ever love me. When we moved, our new town became my bethel. Everything that reminded me of anything bad that had happened to me I placed in a toy chest that I painted to look like the sky, the heavenly coffin of my childhood.

"The complicated sexual map we live amid today does have roots in the past," Daina Ramey Berry and Leslie M. Harris write in *Sexuality and Slavery: Reclaiming Intimate Histories in the Americas.* "Understanding the power dynamics of slavery and their impact on intimacy may give us some clarity with which to view our current condition." Thirty-five percent of African American men are descended from slaves and White men, often their masters.[1] And a third of all molested children are victimized by relatives.[2]

Nell Irvin Painter considered the history of child and sexual abuse within American slave society in "Soul Murder and Slavery," a 1993 lecture at Baylor University. The word "family," she noted, harkens back to the Latin word "familia" (a household) and "famul(us)" (servants or slaves), "deeply embedding the notion of servitude within our concept of family."

The same year that my professor interviewed me, I went to group therapy. I hated that group. I hated when they told me, "It's not your fault." I hated the little embroidered pillow that we passed to each other when it was our turn to talk. I hated how the other women's combined sadness seemed a fraction of my daily rage. I hated how I had to go straight home from our sessions because I was afraid to be in the world, afraid that I might kill someone. I hated how much I thought about those women, all of them older than me, how I told myself that my fellow survivors, betrayed by their fathers and teachers, had it worse. I saw myself in them, never wanted to be them, knew I would become them. I hated how I couldn't hear the word "survivor" without seeing their faces and at the same time doubted they were the picture of survival. I hated how much I needed and loved them.

WOMEN WHO ARE SEXUALLY ASSAULTED HOLD THE TRAUMA IN their bodies, in their wombs, my midwife told me. That's one in five Black women.[3] The trauma can prolong the birthing process, she warned. Sure enough, both my pregnancies stalled. The past working against my unborn children now too, beating back the future.

The midwife caught my second baby, but my first was delivered by an MD. I was referred to Dr. Randolph by my husband's boss, who was referred by her OB-GYN when he retired. "I just want to let you know that she's Black," the retiring doctor told Dennis's employer. "I don't know if you mind." She didn't mind and neither did I. Dr. Randolph was Harvard and Columbia educated and a woman. I eagerly shared my medical history with her: the sexual abuse, the rape, the abortion, that I was in recovery from alcoholism, and the long history of fibroids and hysterectomies in my family. My mother, grandmother, great-grandmother, and sisters all had fibroids and suffered from the painful periods and eventual hysterectomies that went hand in hand with these noncancerous tumors. Sixty percent of Black women are diagnosed with fibroids by age thirty-five, and we are four times more likely to have hysterectomies than White women.[4] Untreated or undetected, these tumors can even be deadly; Rebecca Lee Crumpler, the first Black woman to earn a medical degree in the United States, died from fibroid tumors in 1895. Fibroids can be small as sweet peas or big as full-term babies. My sister's was the size of a grapefruit when they removed it and her womb.

When I became pregnant and told Dr. Randolph that I wanted to have a drug-free childbirth, she said that was fine by her as long as I was not in distress during labor and the baby remained healthy. Those were my goals too: Keep my body out of distress. Keep my baby healthy. She never asked, "Why would you want to feel all of that pain?" the way so many other people did.

If she had, perhaps I would have told her that I saw this pain as one of choice, of power, the natural power of my womb, an initiation by fire that was not a punishment for sinning but a triumph of loving and living, the height of freedom, the freest I would ever be. I wanted to feel the pain of childbirth because it was different from suffering; it was the beginning of everything. I had been numb for too long. Maybe I didn't want anything between my child and me, a perfect circle, the closest I would come to touching God while I was still breathing. Maybe I intuited that I was having a daughter and that soon her body would no longer be her body because everyone would think they had a right to it.

But my labor was not what I'd imagined. Even as I contemplated the picture of a pink and red blooming lotus that I'd hung on the wall in my labor room to coax me into a hypnotic state, it slowed. Nothing that I'd prepared worked: drinking labor-inducing herbal teas, sacral and perineal massage, envisioning my cervix opening up like a flower. Nurses marveled at how calm I kept as they came in and out of my room. Several nurses, who weren't actually assigned to me, came to watch me breathe through the contractions. I was something of a curiosity. Eventually, I was given the synthetic hormone Pitocin to jump-start my labor and an epidural block to numb the pain. Dezi arrived just after midnight.

When it came time to nurse, Dezi seemed too sleepy and was having trouble latching onto my breast. The hospital's lactation nurse, whom I had already paid for, never showed up. A trip to the pediatrician confirmed my worst fear: that my baby was starving.

Maybe if I had been less calm, someone would have noticed I needed help sooner. Maybe my calmness played into the persistent stereotype that Black women are impervious to pain, a lie that can be traced back to the mothers of gynecology: Lucy, Anarcha, Betsey, and many unnamed enslaved Black women were experimented on repeatedly without anesthesia to aid in the invention of the modern speculum. Black women in the United States are four times more likely to die from childbirth-related complications than White women in this country, which already has the worst maternal mortality rate in the industrialized world.[5] In New Jersey, we are seven times more likely to die. The Garden State is one of the most dangerous places in the United States for a Black woman to give birth, no matter how much money she has, how much education, how much support from family.[6]

"Some researchers theorize that a lifelong exposure to racism, combined with limited access to medical resources and a lower overall quality of care, might help explain this disparity in fibroid diagnoses," Dr. Hilda Hutcherson wrote in the *New York Times* in 2020. (She and Dr. Randolph used to have a practice together.) The article was called "Black Women Are Hit Hardest by Fibroid Tumors and Experts Don't Know Why." As the only woman in four generations who has not had a hysterectomy as the result of fibroids, I somehow dodged a generational and societal bullet.

CHAPTER 4

EVERYTHING
THE MOUTH EATS

I always get a little bit sicker before I get better.

The *Sinus Survival* book I'd been reading said chronic conditions like mine are linked to repressed anger and suggested punching a heavy bag or a pillow for release.

Crocuses were pushing through the ground at the base of the enormous maple in our front yard, but I was holed up in my office, hiding from the pollen, staring at the computer. It was my thirty-eighth birthday. An essay I'd written earlier in the year had finally been published, with my maiden name in the byline. I hadn't seen my "real" name in print in over a decade. Ford: a shallow place in a river or stream allowing one to walk or drive across.

It was Grandma Lillie Mae who told me that Josephine took her mother's last name, Burton, because she didn't want anything to do with her White father. The French general Thomas-Alexandre Dumas, who inspired his son's novel *The Count of Monte Cristo*, did the same thing. Born in Saint-Domingue to a French White man and an enslaved woman, Dumas was an American according to the French, and in that context "American" was synonymous with man of color.[1] It was usually the other way around, the White part of the family not wanting anything to do with the Black ones they'd sired. Josephine seemed bold and sure.

I read my essay and my old name about a dozen times, replaying a terse exchange with my neighbor a few days before about the difference between immigrants and slaves, then I typed into Google everything I knew about Josephine: her parents' last names—Burton and Stuart—and where they'd lived in Mississippi—Ocean Springs. Then Google took the parts of my equation and spit out a solid product: the "Col. W. R. Stuart family" photograph.[2] I froze, staring at the photo until my eyes and mouth watered. After a decade spent taking genealogy courses, chasing down birth and death certificates that offered drips of information but never broke through the brick wall of 1870—the first census that listed formerly enslaved people by name, not just as tick marks and property—it was overpowering to see my ancestors embodied. Some Indigenous cultures believe that pictures steal the soul of the ones who are photographed. But on that day, my birthday, the picture did the opposite: it breathed something into me.

The Colonel and his wife, Elizabeth, were the same shade of white. Tempy was almost black, the girls she had likely made with the Colonel somewhere between. Tempy's dark face was illuminated on a diagonal, with tight curls around her head like a halo; she had a straight mouth, and eyes that gave nothing away. It looked like she had a kerchief on her head, reminiscent of the tignons Creole women were forced to wear as a sign of their lower status in colonial New Orleans. She, Elizabeth, and the two girls were serious. The Colonel was slightly smiling.

The picture told our family's story, our country's story, and a biblical story in one frame.

Tempy was the Hagar of Genesis, an enslaved African woman, the first person in the Bible to name God. Like Hagar, my great-great-grandmother was enslaved to a woman who couldn't have any children. When that woman married, my great-great-grandmother was given to her and her new husband as a wedding gift, and out of this offering Tempy would bring six children into the world. Hagar brought forth Ishmael.

The photograph told a thousand stories. The story of every person in the picture. The story of why they'd gathered. The story of how they each somehow belonged to one another. There was the story of their clothes, their Sunday best it seems, and the story of the porch they were seated on, those hurricane windows, that home. It looked the way I had imagined it.

The picture of my ancestors was taken in the early 1890s, twenty-five years after slavery ended. Almost every time I look at it, I wonder why Tempy would pose for what amounted to a family portrait with the couple who stole her freedom. Were her eyes sad or stoic? Was there something akin to love between Tempy and the Colonel or had it been nothing more than a series of rapes? What did Elizabeth, the woman Tempy served for most of her life, feel about it all? Mostly, I want desperately to know that Tempy experienced pleasure, and knew love.

Berry and Harris ask in *Sexuality and Slavery*: "What was possible in terms of emotional and sexual intimacy under slavery? How were enslaved people able to form families amid a system that limited autonomy so dramatically and violently? Could relationships between enslaved people and enslavers entail non-abusive emotional intimacy?" There are no easy answers. Not enough is known about the private lives of enslaved women, partly because of what historian Darlene Clark Hine calls dissemblance, "the behavior and attitudes of Black women that created the appearance of openness and disclosure but actually shielded the truth of their inner lives and selves from their oppressor."[3] Enslaved women wore the mask. Dissemblance was about self-preservation. Hine suggests it developed because of rape and the threat of rape—constants in the lives of Black women.

Because the photo was from so long after the end of slavery, I feel that Tempy must have had a choice. But maybe she didn't think she did. It can take so much time for my logical mind to catch up with my physical reality. The trauma of a lifetime of enslavement and of bearing children for her enslaver may have frozen her in place. *The Body Keeps the Score* calls this "immobilization" or "freeze response." The workbook for *Adult Children of Alcoholics* calls this "trauma bonding."

Master and slave. Man and wife. All that I've learned about love adds up to dominance and the wrong kind of belonging.

Outside of my office, I could see my husband talking to a friend while our daughters ran in circles around the maple and its exposed roots, knobby as the ginger I was drinking daily for health and mental clarity. Part of me wanted to shout wildly out the window, "I've found my people!" Another part told me to keep quiet. The flatness of the picture matched me. I didn't know if I had the capacity to love my daughters the way they deserved, or anyone really. I didn't know if I wanted to stay married. I didn't know if I could trust my thinking. I didn't know how to explain what I was feeling. Deep obsession with your ancestors is called progonoplexia. Not having words for your emotions is called alexithymia.

"Wise men and women in the indigenous world argue that humans are cursed by the language they possess, or that possess them," Malidoma Patrice Somé writes in *The Healing Wisdom of Africa*. "For indigenous people, to utter means two things: first, it signifies nostalgia for a true home, because language tempts us with the possibility of returning home to meaning. . . . Second, to utter means to be in exile." Sorrowful and sweet, everything the mouth eats.

Marriage and children had not ended my dispossession or my longing.

I STARTED DRINKING IN BRAZIL, ON AN EXCHANGE PROGRAM, when I was sixteen years old. Grandpa Martin had been dead six months and my father was newly sober. I had vowed that I would never be like my dad in that way. But by sophomore year of college, I was drinking way too much. One morning I woke with my red dress hitched up above my hips, my underwear down around my ankles, and a guy I remembered trying to avoid the night before in bed next to me. So, I tried to stop.

Sobering up is like thawing out if you've gone numb, a siege of pins and needles. The longer you've been on ice, the more painful it is. That is how the memory snuck up on me:

Sunny, middle of the day, in the best part of autumn, when I could still go outside with no jacket, the air so crisp and filled with the scent of pine and cedar that it stung, but just a little. I used to love the fall. I used to love my relative. I don't remember what he said to get my pants off of me, if he cajoled me or not—he was big and I was small. I do remember how my private felt like it was on fire, how my favorite ribbed turtleneck matched the bright leaves on the big oak outside, how the changing season crept in through the thick panels hanging from my parent's bedroom windows, one slightly cracked to let in some of the clean Pine Barrens air.

THE YEAR THAT I RETURNED FROM BRAZIL, RESEARCHERS FROM the National Institute of Mental Health began the first ever long-term study of the impact of sexual abuse on female development. As late as 1974, the *Comprehensive Textbook of Psychiatry* considered incest extremely rare and maybe even beneficial to its victims. "The vast majority of them were none the worse for the experience," the textbook said. In eerie similarity, proponents of slavery had said that abusive masters were rare, that slavery was good for Black people.

After following the girls for twenty-five years, the study results showed that, compared to their peers, sexually abused girls across race and social circumstance suffered more depression, cognitive deficits, dissociative symptoms, and troubled sexual development. They had more major illnesses and health-care utilization, abnormal stress-hormone responses, persistent post-traumatic stress disorder, premature deliveries, and drug and alcohol abuse.[4]

Three months before my twenty-second birthday, my college graduation, and the discovery in lower Manhattan of the oldest and largest known burial ground on the continent for free and enslaved Africans, I took my last drink. I also discovered capoeira. If you are a Black person in this world, capoeira is a road map for keeping your sanity. Part dance, part martial art, part spiritual program for living wrapped in African cosmology, it holds truth and myth, speaks to one and performs the other.

Capoeira was carried across the Atlantic from West Africa or created by Africans once they arrived in Brazil in bondage. Either way, it was a way for the enslaved in Brazil to protect themselves, maintain their culture, find freedom. For obvious reasons, the enslaved were not allowed to practice self-defense, so they would form a circle of privacy and practice inside of it. To the slaveholders, the singing and drumming looked like fun and games, but that ginga step, samba in slow motion, was preparation for a kick, the swaying arms might become a blow, and before he knew it, a master could lose his life. To keep theirs, the newly self-liberated might head to the hinterlands to establish their own quilombo, or fugitive slave community. Many of today's capoeira schools carry the name of the largest of such communities, Palmares.

No place in the New World enslaved more Africans than Brazil or for longer. After three and a half centuries, it was the last country to abolish slavery in 1888. After it was outlawed, so too was capoeira. Anyone caught playing it, or any of its instruments, could end up in jail, or with a sliced Achilles tendon, or dead. The ban was lifted in the mid-twentieth century, but capoeira stayed tucked away, like Blackness. Now capoeira is Brazil's national sport and practiced all over the world. But in the year I lived in Brazil, I never heard of the art form. And I almost never saw other Black people, though the country has the largest Black population outside of Africa. Only two, in all those months: a twentysomething who worked in the local record store and a reporter who came to interview me about the exchange program.

Brazil felt, to me, like the United States inverted: In the United States, any amount of Black made you Black. In Brazil, any amount of White made you anything but Black. The town where I lived was a reverse Ellis Island. Santa Bárbara d'Oeste was founded by American Confederates at the end of the Civil War. During my year there, I lived with two families in town and a third on the sugar plantation at the city's edge. Every year, the Confederate descendants host a party in the cemetery where their ancestors are buried. They dress up in *Gone with the Wind*–style costumes, eat fried chicken and apple pie, and waltz with effervescence on a concrete dance floor emblazoned with the stars and bars. I was at the first party that they opened to the public, and that was where I saw my first Confederate monument up close.

The confederados introduced pecans, private Protestant schools, and state-of-the-art plows to Brazil. They showed their new countrymen how to turn sugar into pinga, a potent rum. The first time I tried it, I had one too many shots and fell out of my chair. I had mostly fallen out of touch with my body by then. Friends sometimes had to remind me to breathe. I'd forget where I was, spatially, and they would have to yell at me to stop walking on their feet. I'd forget to eat, and fainted once because of it. The *Twelve Steps of Adult Children* workbook says that "disconnection from our body represents a disconnection from our real identity."

When I learned about capoeira, from a TV special while I was in college, everything about the art appealed to me. It was a holistic practice; it fed my hunger for physical strength, for music, and for spiritual connection to Africa and the lost stories of my ancestors. It's what I went to Brazil looking for in the first place—connection, strength, some sense of myself. It took almost a decade, but in 1999, I somehow managed to find a capoeira class in the city.

By the time the first session of the class rolled around, I was newly pregnant and already in the throes of morning sickness. I didn't want to do anything to jeopardize the baby's health. But the call to Brazil was strong. It was like I'd left something of myself there that needed to be collected. Drums call the spirit, wake up anything dead. So I went to a Brazilian drumming class instead. I slapped the shit out of the caixa hanging from a strap around my neck, and I felt so alive on the one hand, so ill on the other. My first-trimester nausea was as strong as my deep longing, what the Brazilians call saudades.

In Montclair, seven years later, the length of a spiritual cycle, the age a slave child would be put to work, the number of veils to be lifted before enlightenment, the timing was just right. It was 2006, the same year Tarana Burke started saying "Me Too" while working with sexually abused black and brown girls. In my town's high school auditorium, I learned how to ginga—capoeira's fundamental footwork—and how to turn a cartwheel into self-defense. I knew how to kick from years of cheerleading, dancing, some tae kwon do, tons of kickboxing. The escapes were the hard part. Tabletop, squat or lunge away from an incoming foot, then cartwheel and kick back while you're upside down. It was not methodical, or mechanical. It was all rhythm, all flow. The escapes were beautiful.

On the last night of the adult school class, I summoned enough courage to play in the roda. I stepped inside the circle, crouched down in front of the musicians facing Gaivota, my teacher and opponent. We briefly clasped hands, then cartwheeled toward the middle. At first I mimicked his moves, but as the music played and I found my stride, I spun and lunged in and out of trouble, before cartwheeling away with a timid kick back while standing on my hands. Upside down in the aú or in a handstand—that's when you're closest to your ancestors. When you're walking on your hands, you're walking with your dead.

The capoeira circle has no beginning or end. Capoeira has no winners or losers. A kick to the body is called a blessing. The point is not to punch an opponent into submission, but to play and beguile, not to block a blow but to negate it. While we played-danced-fought, everyone sang. "You cannot lie and make music," the trauma expert Van der Kolk said on a podcast about family secrets. "Music is a kind of truth telling."[5] The interest in more classes was so intense that the instructor had started up an Afro-Brazilian arts school in town by fall. The academy's walls were painted the pastel colors of the Pelourinho neighborhood in Salvador, Bahia. In our uniforms, never stagnant, always moving, we were like a white flowing river.

Gaivota told us that when enslaved Africans arrived in Bahia, Brazil, their captors would walk them through an elaborate underground maze for hours to disorient them, fearing that if the enslaved knew how close they were to the ocean, they'd try to swim back home. The story reminded me of a resistance to slavery off the coast of Georgia known as Igbo Landing, when a group of captive Africans marched into the sea. They preferred drowning to slavery. According to one legend, the Igbo walked across the water. According to another, the one that Toni Morrison made famous in *Song of Solomon*, they flew over it.

"The folklore of black people centers on the ability of the weak to survive through cunning, trickery, and sheer deception in an environment of the strong and the powerful," theologian James Cone wrote in *God of the Oppressed*. In the hulls of slave ships, stolen from different tribes with different tongues, African people could not speak to each other, could not comfort one another, could not ask, "Where do you think they're taking us?" or pray together that their families would never forget them. They could not communicate with language, so they crafted instead—spirituals, capoeira—and in crafting left us a common language of survival.

WHEN IT CAME TIME FOR OUR BATIZADO, AN ANNUAL INITIATION ritual for new capoeira students, my daughters received their green cords and nicknames but I didn't join the ceremony. I'd had sinus surgery, because the allergies I'd recently developed made it harder for me to breathe every spring and every fall, and I think I used the operation as an excuse. I told myself I wasn't ready to be baptized. I'd

scored at the top of my class at the little test our teacher had
given us at the end of the session, and from my right side,
I could get into a handstand and take a few quick upside-
down steps. But I couldn't do it from the left. "There is no
bad side" of the body, Gaivota says. "There's just one side
you don't love as much as the other." And that is the rub,
those bad sides. I really wanted a nickname, but what is
more bonding than a nickname? Batizado felt serious, like
a commitment, another surrender.

Surrender is the first step in AA, the hardest one to
take. My first sponsor told me that the military definition
of surrender is to go over to the winning side. The same
description sums up the negativa, capoeira's foundational
defensive move. To lunge away from a jab or kick is like not
fighting. It's like giving up. It's like what a nun once told
me about meditation: not to push anything away—not the
garbage truck beeping while it backs up or the dogs barking
or even my thoughts about what I need to do later in the
day. "Let them all in," she said. "Let them say whatever it is
they need to say."

In the surrender, down on the ground, bottomed out,
everything becomes possible.

"Everything the mouth eats" is what capoeira was to
Mestre Pastinha, founding father of Capoeira Angola.
Mestre Bimba founded Capoeira Regional, the other of the
art's two main styles, and he kept a list of rules tacked to
the wall of his academy: "Do not drink." "Always keep your
body relaxed." "Don't be afraid of getting closer to your opponent. The closer you can get to him, the more you will

learn." Audre Lorde said something similar about anger, that it's loaded with information and energy, an arsenal potentially useful against oppression, its object change.

Underneath my anger is usually some kind of grief.

That terse exchange with my neighbor that I was thinking about when I decided to google my ancestors' names is an everything-the-mouth-eats story.

The tree roots on our block buckled the sidewalks. Days before I came across the photograph of my ancestors, I was trying to find some even ground to stand on while waiting for the school bus to deposit my daughter when my neighbor also waiting asked, "Are you going to the protest?" In the wake of Hurricane Katrina, as immigrants poured into New Orleans to help rebuild the city, the House responded with legislation to punish undocumented people, and immigration rallies had erupted all over the country. Meanwhile, two years after the hurricane, my uncle's NOLA house, formerly my grandmother's, remained storm damaged and unlivable, but he was living in it anyway. I tried hard not to roll my eyes when I told her I was too busy to go the rally but didn't succeed.

"But we're all immigrants," she said, "all of us in this country." Then she asked me where my parents were from and where their parents were from. "They weren't from the islands?"

I thought of the college colleague who had refused to believe that my people weren't from the Caribbean like his, because, he told me as we walked back to campus from Columbus Circle, I didn't act like an American Black.

I thought of Mrs. Sauer's flag assignment, my dad retorting, "Who's more American than us?" I thought of all the newscasters on the airwaves saying what my neighbor was about to say, that slaves were immigrants too, ignoring their forced migration.

There is a violence in misnaming things. There is a violence in always holding back.

"He who cannot howl will not find his pack," Charles Simic wrote in his poem "Ax." I didn't growl exactly when I told my neighbor that my people were from a continent.

I am dressed for Carnaval at the sugar cane factory, Santa Barbara d'Oeste, 1986.

CHAPTER 5

PARADISE LOST

The Fords moved to New Orleans from Mississippi in 1946, after the war ended and my Grandpa Martin was laid off from his job at Keesler Air Force Base in Biloxi. Grandma Lillie Mae was a good saver, so they were able to buy a two-story shotgun in what my dad called a Black pocket of the Irish Channel, on Josephine Street. This should have been a good omen. But not long after the Fords arrived, the whole area was razed to expand the Whites-only Saint Thomas projects, which became known, later, for being the most violent housing project in the country. So the family moved to a smaller shotgun in Tremé, across the street from Congo Square, where the enslaved had congregated on Sundays and free women of color once bought up property.

In 1953, the Ford home on Tremé's Saint Claude Street was demolished to make way for Louis Armstrong Park and Dad's family was displaced again. My grandmother wound up in the back-of-town, used-to-be swampland, on a street named for the Sun King's first and favorite illegitimate daughter, the Princess of Conti.

I still can't shake the images of New Orleanians stranded on their roofs, clinging to the shingles for dear life, doors of boarded-up houses with numbers and signs spray-painted in bright colors on them like homicidal hieroglyphics: *Katrina was here. The house has been checked. This is how many people were found dead.* Police officers lined up across a bridge with guns raised to keep Katrina victims at bay, and White vigilantes gunning down Black men just trying to cross to higher ground at Algiers Point. That's where slaves were corralled before being sold to colonists. It's where Grandma Lillie Mae lived now.

Rows of FEMA trailers clustered together like a first-circle-of-hell welcoming committee at the foot of the Crescent City Connection bridge, our path to Grandma's nursing home. Their tin tops stuck out above a concrete wall sprayed with the words "Paradise Lost" and "Kill=Aid." None of it was the homecoming I'd imagined. All I saw was a watery world that had tried to drown my family more than once. The Gulf, the Mississippi—they were once a single giant mass, and New Orleans was the silt beneath. Maybe all these water events are just the river remembering where it used to be, like Toni Morrison said, and trying to reunite its broken family.

Water has a perfect memory, Morrison wrote. So does the body. Someday, my teeth will return to the way they were before braces, the front four slotted and spaced, the gaps signs of wisdom.

On all of the trips to New Orleans I'd taken before, I'd never thought of all that the water had seen: plantation mansions rising up from sugarcane fields along the shore, egrets dancing with their long stick legs on the levee as slave ships docked to sell their cargo. One such ship, the *Barque Pioneer*, came all the way from the port of Baltimore carrying twenty persons of color, an eleven-year-old boy among them, "to be sold, disposed of as slaves, or held in service" by their owner, my great-great-grandfather, Colonel Stuart.[1]

Grandma's nursing home sat like a thrown-out pizza box at the edge of Algiers, a satellite section of the larger city. I'd pictured something grander for her. At least the facility had had enough warning and resources to move all of its residents to Baton Rouge in anticipation of the storm. Algiers suffered only minor damage from Katrina. A month afterward, Grandma and her fellow residents moved back there.

It was the first time I'd ever seen Grandma's real hair. Normally, it was hidden under a wig. Now, the silver strands so tightly woven together turned her head into a grid.

"The ladies at the nursing home did it for me," she said, proudly passing her hand over her head and smiling. They'd done her nails too. She stretched out her fingers as much as she could so I could appreciate them, a red brighter than the bougainvillea decorating the veranda where we were gathered and much better manicured than my own. My hair was also in braids, and it was sobering to see myself in the contours of my grandmother's face for the first time—same broad cheeks, sloped mouth—as she was bending toward the end of life.

My soles were burning from standing on the veranda's concrete slab in thin sandals and my daughter's cheeks were already red. Everyone was wilting from the heat. We decided to go back to Lillie Mae's air-conditioned room, and Dezi pushed Grandma's wheelchair through the fluorescent hallway with all the strength in her seven-year-old arms.

"That's Devany, and Desiree," Lillie Mae said. She had only ever met Desiree, but she recognized the girls and Dennis from the pictures I sent every Christmas. Her mind was sharp, and sometimes so was her tongue. My father had always told me that the lighter your skin was, the higher the chances were that Lillie Mae would like you. My daughters had the creamy skin and wavy hair my grandmother favored. Like Dad and Grandpa.

Grandma was having a hard time hearing me, but I tried to tell her the things I had learned, continuing a conversation we had started years before: Tempy was born around 1821, just like Harriet Tubman, and lived to be 104 years old. She was enslaved to Elizabeth McCauley's family and when Elizabeth married Colonel W. R. Stuart, Tempy was given to the couple as a present. A newspaper reported that Tempy was the oldest person in Jackson County at the time of her death and that three ministers, "two white," attended her funeral—she had to have been held in esteem.[2]

"Tempy? She was our cousin," my grandmother said. "Tempy and Al Smith. They were famous musicians and they moved to New York." Grandma, it turns out, had known Tempy and the Colonel's granddaughter and great-grandson, Tempy Elizabeth and Al. I'd seen a picture of the Smiths on the same website where I'd found the Stuart family photo. In it, Tempy Elizabeth is seated at a baby grand piano, flanked by her son, Al, and the rest of her children.

I asked but Grandma didn't answer if she ever got to hear the Smith cousins play. She just beamed and repeated, "The Smiths. Tempy and Al were famous musicians," like a mantra, the kind I try when I can't get to sleep. It seemed to comfort her, and I imagined and also understood that there was a special security in being attached to her husband's sprawling clan full of siblings and cousins, since she had none.

The musical Tempy was born to the first Tempy's son Alfred. His progeny were my distant cousins. The Colonel's "Black descendants," as the website described Alfred's family, lived primarily in New York. I knew I had to find these Black descendants. One of them, Renee Smith, had donated all the photos that appeared on the site along with family letters, newspaper clippings, and census reports to the Alfred Burton Stuart Family collection archived at the University of Southern Mississippi. The research there confirmed what Grandpa Martin had told me, that Elizabeth was sick and couldn't have any children while Tempy had plenty. Along with Alfred, Tempy had had another son, Warren, and three daughters, Violet, May, and Pauline. They all were listed in Jackson County's educable index, a kind of census for school-age children. But there was no mention of my great-grandmother, Josephine.

I'd learned about the Colonel too. Born in 1820 in Kent County, Maryland, Stuart made his way to Baton Rouge in 1840. By the time he was thirty, he held fifty-nine slaves, a sugar plantation, and real estate valued at $20,000—about $600,000 today.

The Colonel's "Valuable Sugar Plantation" was located in West Baton Rouge Parish, "about 120 miles from New Orleans on the bank of the Mississippi River." An ad he placed in January 1853 said his plantation produced about five hundred thousand pounds of sugar that year. "There are about fifty acclimated Negroes, most of whom are No. 1 hands having been selected within the last three years from gangs of Maryland and Virginia Negroes," he wrote. "There are Mules and Carts enough to take off a large crop. . . . The Terms will be 1, 2 and 3 years for the land and 1 and 2 years credit for the Negroes."

I looked up what "acclimated" might mean in this context. Either they were acclimated to the heat, "broken in" and ready to work, or they had already been exposed to yellow fever and were considered immune.

So much harder to kick than alcohol, just as beloved, just as deadly, sugar runs in my family: from my great-great-grandfather to the more recent generations of men struck with diabetes. My father has it. My uncle died of complications from it after both of his legs were amputated. My grandmother was widowed because of it, leaving my mother fatherless at seven. Her father, Nathaniel, wasn't overweight. He was slim and taut as a stick of cane. "He died of sugar," my grandmother Louise told me. Afterward, Granny married Alonzo Walton and they opened up Walton's Trailer Park and Grocery Store, but my siblings and I called it a candy store. That's what people really went there for. It had a glass case filled with Slim Jims, licorice laces, wrapped caramels, two-cent Bazooka bubble gum, and candy bars named for the baseball star of the moment. My favorite was the round chocolate and caramel, "Reggie." As long as I ate my lunch and dinner and minded Granny, I was allowed to eat candy from the store whenever I wanted, and I did.

I try to avoid sugar now, an extra stressor on my already stressed, overreacting, allergic immune system, but it is everywhere, in everything. You can have sugar, you can give sugar. You can be sugar. To not eat sugar in New Orleans seemed like a sacrilege.

I had been to visit Lillie Mae in New Orleans a few months after I got engaged. My plan was to spend nights with my cousin Nikkie and days with our grandmother in her house on Conti, learning what I could about our family. But the whole trip tested my patience. Because of the state of her house, the result of years of hoarding, and Grandma's acerbic nature, trying to get information out of her and that place was dispiriting. I'd get itchy from her couch, more cat hair than cushion, or nauseous from a smell somewhere deep in the barrel of her home, or put out by her comments: "You look just like your momma," she said when she greeted me. "Have you put on some weight?" In her front room, Grandma showed me a glass trimmed with gold that had belonged to maybe an aunt of hers who had worked as a maid for some wealthy people. But she barely let my fingers graze the trim or the inscribed date, nineteen-oh-something, before she swiftly returned it to the curio cabinet bound by a padlocked chain. All I left with from that visit was a distaste for Grandma's house, an indecipherable tape recording, and a few notes scribbled on my reporter's pad, the names Tempy and Josephine in the margins.

I'd cut our interviews short and take myself to the light-filled rooms at the New Orleans Museum of Art, Anne Rice's mansion in the Garden District, Marie Laveau's House of Voodoo, the Audubon Zoo. My uncle treated me to a po' boy sandwich and I treated myself to a bag of beignets from a street vendor near the river. The only real food I had was Nikki's boiled crawfish, which we ate straight from the pot in her kitchen. Mostly I spent my time driving up and down the causeway, crossing Lake Pontchartrain, looking for a fucking green salad. This was before there was a Whole Foods on every corner, and I could not manage to find fresh vegetables. The salads at restaurants in the city were too expensive and I didn't want to sit down to order one.

New Orleans seemed at once to love me and be bent on destroying me and my family. If the storms didn't get the Fords, the sugar would. Both the man who first granulated sugar in the United States and the man who invented the machine to refine sugar into crystals were from the city, one a Creole and the other among the gens de couleur.

In "the city of the world where you can eat and drink the most and suffer the least," enslaved people were malnourished.[3] "I went out every morning to see the slaves at breakfast in the quarters," Eliza Potter wrote in her memoir about her time working among New Orleans's rich planter families. "And, to my astonishment, I did not see any of them have anything for the whole week but a pint cup of buttermilk and a slice of bread, those who could not take buttermilk, had a cup of coffee, made of browned corn, sweetened with molasses. I never saw meat of any kind given them while I was there." Fresh fruit and vegetables were hard to come by.

On the sugar plantations, miles away, enslaved people could live with relatives in their own spaces and grow their own food. In cities, enslaved people were more isolated, usually living in the same buildings with their enslavers, or in dwellings erected in the courtyards, like compounds. I heard someone say in a meeting once that isolation is the highest form of control. The living arrangements in New Orleans "intensified relations between slave women and their owners."[4] The 1860 slave schedule shows Tempy living with the Colonel and Elizabeth in New Orleans in the same house. Two other bonded people lived there too: "Black, female, 14 and 15." Who were they, I wonder, and what happened to them? I wonder, too, if Tempy offered herself up to protect these young girls.

Tempy moved to New Orleans with the Colonel and Elizabeth when the couple married in 1858. The Colonel had sold his sugar plantation and was working and trading on the cotton exchange. The same month he and Elizabeth celebrated their second wedding anniversary, Tempy had her first child by him, Alfred. Five of Tempy's children by the Colonel were born in New Orleans. Some slaveholders became their own slave brokers, fathering children with their enslaved women to sell them. The Colonel never did.

When he retired, the Colonel and his wife settled in the Mississippi Gulf town that he was credited with publicizing as a vacation spot, and that's where my father, his father, and his grandmother were all born, in Ocean Springs. No longer enslaved, Tempy settled there, too, working for the Stuarts as their cook. The Colonel also kept working. In Ocean Springs, he became a gentleman farmer, raising oranges, sheep, and pecans. He became a father for the sixth and final time when Tempy gave birth to Josephine.

NEW ORLEANS WAS THE BIGGEST SLAVE MARKET IN THE COUNtry in 1848, when the *Pioneer* docked here. After Saint-Domingue's slaves rebelled, defeated Napoleon's army, and claimed independence for their new country, Haiti,

Congress abolished the transatlantic slave trade, but slaves could still be bought and sold domestically. The importance of an enslaved woman was her capacity to give birth. "Natural increase," and not importation of slaves, explained the enormous growth of the slave population; the domestic slave trade was fueled by rape and forced reproduction. The French Quarter and Algiers, the city's oldest and second-oldest neighborhoods, respectively, were the market's center. But I didn't see a single sign to memorialize the trade on which the city was built.

In the Colonel's day, a visit to the auction block was as much an outing as an evening at the opera. The marble-floored lobby of the old Saint Louis Hotel had a slave pen in the center of it, under a domed ceiling that let in shafts of light. Visitors could take tea while auctioneers sold children away from their mothers and commanded up to $35,000 in today's money for "fancy girls"—light-skinned ones with good hair.[5] European colonists couldn't get their women to come to Louisiana's disease-infested swamps. So they entered the equivalent of common-law marriages with the native women they encountered, then the African slaves they imported, creating a cascade of colored people and a new kind of kin, left-handed families. But when the colony became American, "one drop" came into effect. "One drop" of Black blood meant Black, meant slave. Racial varieties had to be identified and codified. The "fancy girls" got fancy names. Octoroon. Quadroon. Mulatto. The Colonel would have confronted them all as he walked the streets to his office on Carondelet.

Those streets have seen my father's first date, my first hair pressing, my family traipsing over to church on Easter together, Nikkie and me trading lipstick, her ducking catcalls like a capoeira mestre, me sightseeing and sipping at something syrupy and chemical blue that I pestered my brother's girlfriend into buying. Those streets have seen the evolution of my body—when it was seven and still mine, when it was fourteen and still growing and I hated it, was always trying to change it, when I was nineteen and abandoned it, when I was twenty-seven and engaged to be married and just beginning to get it back.

When I was in my earlier twenties, I started modeling to make extra money while I was freelance writing. I contracted with an agency that specialized in body parts and they got me jobs modeling shoes for Yves Saint Laurent and Anne Klein, jeans by a Swedish designer, and underwear made in Japan. The owner sent me to a consultant who specialized in sizing you up and telling you what to do to make yourself more of a commodity. She found a lot of problems: my height (too short), my hair (too frizzy), my butt. "It sticks out too much," she said. This was not news to me. My high school track coach had nicknamed me "Shelf Butt." Consequently, the consultant prescribed butt-reducing exercises. I did those religiously for the next month until I found a full-time job as a reporter, and sometimes did them even after that.

An editor at the newspaper wanted me to write about it all, but I could not make the words sing. I sensed that he was looking for a feel-good feature, but as soon as I started to write about walking back and forth in front of people and trying to offer myself up well enough that they would pay me, I'd become beleaguered and fatigued. Who wanted to read about me standing in purple underwear in an abandoned warehouse in northern New Jersey while three people inspected the stretch marks on my upper thigh and butt, and discussed them first in Japanese, then in English, with strained voices?

Cattle. Mulatto. Mule of the world.

When I took pictures of my daughters in their Mardi Gras masks on Bourbon Street, they vamped for the camera and I soaked it up, telling them how cute they were, how sweet. I still don't know when they learned how to do that.

"Come give me some sugar," my parents always say to my children.

"I could just eat you up," my grandparents would say in the presence of cuteness, baby cheeks, and we girls knew that this was our goal, to be delectable. Long after I outgrew soles as soft as ripe plums, I still aimed to be consumed.

CHAPTER 6

PASSING STRANGE

My daughters were digging holes around the perimeter of our first garden and I was going behind them, filling the little tombs they made with bright marigolds, when Dad phoned to say, "Grandma is failing." His voice was shaky just like when I was a teenager and I heard him talking about his sick father on the other side of my bedroom wall. She died the next day.

Grandma's funeral was held at the newly combined First Grace Methodist Church in New Orleans. It was a sanctuary in progress, with folding chairs standing in for pews, paint swatches lined up behind the altar, and peeling plaster. Lillie Mae had been a longtime member of the 155-year-old Grace United Methodist Church on Iberville in the Ninth

Ward until the storm blew out parts of its walls. That mostly Black church then moved in with the mostly White First Methodist on Canal, and the two became First Grace. In the choir, a Black woman in a fancy hat and a younger White woman in a peasant skirt and Birkenstocks belted out a spiritual that I'd never heard. I wondered what Grandma would have thought of that girl's open toes in church.

To the best of her knowledge, Lillie Mae Ford (née Daniel) was born on August 3, 1910, somewhere in Mississippi. She never had a birth certificate, never knew her parents, who died when she was an infant, and lived most of her life in New Orleans.

By the time I was born, my grandparents were living in separate homes, but they never officially divorced. Their only daughter, Shirley, was born in 1932. She seemed like a healthy baby, but when she was around eighteen months old she started having seizures and stopped developing mentally. She couldn't communicate in any way and, when she was ten, she had an accident that left her unable to walk. My grandmother cared for her at home and tried to get her admitted to the State Colony and Training School, but the institution refused her because it felt she posed "too much of a hazard to the other inmates." Shirley lost most of her teeth, was convulsing several times a day, and urinating and defecating on herself in the process. With four other children at home, Shirley's care had become too much for Grandma. And so, in 1948, she was committed to East Louisiana State Hospital. When it had opened a hundred years earlier, the hospital was known as the "Insane Asylum for the State of Louisiana," and it treated all kinds of so-called mental defectives, from alcoholics and fallen women to schizophrenics and "imbeciles," Shirley's classification. Richard Avedon photographed its patients for the book *Nothing Personal,* a collaboration with his schoolmate James Baldwin. By then, the hospital symbolized all that was wrong with how America treated the mentally ill. But in 1948, it was my grandmother's last hope.

Nine months later, the day before her sixteenth birthday, Shirley died there of status epilepticus, a severe seizure. She likely suffered from a genetic disorder that would come to be known as Angelman syndrome.[1] My father had just started the ninth grade and would have been getting ready for school that morning. He has no memory of being told that his sister had died or of attending her funeral. Dad also had no idea that his grandmother's name was Josephine until I told him, after his mother told me.

JOSEPHINE WAS BORN IN 1875, TEN YEARS AFTER EMANCIPA-tion. I made this discovery on my thirty-ninth birthday. I'd just watched *Passing Strange,* the story of a young Black man from California who realizes himself in a bohemian community in Amsterdam, which reminded me of what I'd hoped to find the year I spent in Brazil, reigniting my longing for the grandmothers I never knew. So I looked up the photo again and sent another email to the author of the website where the picture was posted. Maybe because it was my birthday, or maybe because my ancestors knew I was serious, this time he answered.

He'd lost contact with Renee Smith, the woman who'd donated the photo, but knew she had a cousin, Bob Smith, in Staten Island and suggested I look him up in the phone book. I'd have more luck finding my enslaved ancestors' first and last names listed on the manifest of a ship from Africa than I would finding the right Bob Smith in a New York City telephone directory. I tried my luck instead with "Facebook for the dead," the genealogy website Ancestry.[2] I gifted myself a trial membership, then rubbed my hands together and got to work. Five minutes later, I hit a little jackpot. I found Josephine in the census.

Josephine was thirty-five and married with children in April 1910, when the census was taken. If the newspaper reports were right and Tempy was born around 1821, that would mean she was in her midfifties when she gave birth to Josephine, a good fourteen years after she had Alfred Burton Stuart, her and the Colonel's oldest child. Maybe Grandpa had this part wrong and Josephine was actually Tempy and the Colonel's granddaughter. Then again, I am fourteen years younger than my oldest sibling. Maybe history was just repeating itself.

Tempy wouldn't have had a say in when she started having children, because she was enslaved then, but what about when she stopped? Only her first two kids, Alfred and Violet, were born during slavery, when she was in no position to consent. But Tempy's next four children were born after the Union won the war. When the Colonel returned to her bedroom, long after slavery had ended, when she was supposed to be a free woman, did she consent, relent, or did he just take what he wanted? Perhaps she convinced herself to accept some discomfort now so that her kids would have a better life later, or so the Colonel wouldn't make problems for her, or because it just wasn't prudent to say no. Freedom alongside White people she didn't know might have seemed worse than remaining with the ones she did. The scholar Virginia Meacham Gould writes that "some slave women participated in sexual liaisons with their masters or with other White men or free men of color for the relative or legitimate freedom or social mobility that such relationships could offer." Maybe the Colonel promised her something: property, protection, for her or for the children.

For months, after my family went to bed, I crept into my office for grandma time, their lives coming into relief. I chased the shaking green leaves on Ancestry over Tempy's, Josephine's, and Grandpa Martin's names and clicked, scouring the documents they led to: Josephine's 1894 marriage certificate and more census records that showed her living with her husband, James Ford, a reverend, and, by 1920, their six children. Josephine and James started their family in 1895 with the arrival of their only girl, Rosa Bell. Alfred came next in 1897, followed by Adrian in 1904, my grandpa, Martin, in 1905, Burton, also known as Jack, in 1911, and Clarence in December of 1913. Of all of these siblings, I'd only ever heard mention of Adrian, whom

Grandpa had said was an artist. Perhaps some of his siblings had died prematurely, or perhaps Grandpa's memory was selective. He'd lived in the same small town as his grandmother, Tempy, but had never mentioned her name to me.

The Fords were the only "mulattoes" living on a county road with mostly Black families and one White family in 1920. In the small gridlines of the censuses under the column marked "race," Josephine evolved from mulatto to Black and Grandpa from Negro to colored, the distance shrinking between us. When those leaves stopped shaking, I should have called it quits and gone to bed, but I was hooked. I kept digging. I moved on to the surname message boards.

What I found was a post by "RSmith," who was perhaps Alfred's descendant, Renee: *Tempe was a Louisiana resident— she was the slave of Col. W. R. Stuart and his wife Lizzie McCauley. I am seeking her prior owners and/or her history before she was purchased by the McCauley family as a wedding gift.*

The post was from two years prior, but I felt confident that "RSmith" was diligently looking for her people, would find my response, and get back to me.

IF YOU ARE GOING TO LOOK FOR YOUR ENSLAVED ANCESTORS, you will run up against the limitations of language. When they were "slave and master," my great-great-grandparents had children together, or my great-great-grandmother had children for my great-great-grandfather, or by him. Then they weren't "slave and master," and they had more children together or for or by. Tempy's life challenged my limited understanding of "slavery" and "motherhood," and how to use them properly. "Oppressive language does more than represent violence; it is violence," Toni Morrison said when she accepted the Nobel Prize in literature. "Sexist language, racist language, theistic language—all are typical of the policing languages of mastery, and cannot, do not, permit new knowledge or encourage the mutual exchange of ideas."[3]

I thought of my neighbor, conflating slaves and immigrants, I thought of how I say slave and master and what those words actually convey. I thought of my literary and historic heroes, Toni Morrison, Audre Lorde, Harriet Tubman, Sojourner Truth, all of whom gave themselves new names.

In her book *Sisters in the Wilderness*, Delores Williams writes that the way to claim experience is to name it. The photo of my ancestors was captioned the "Col. Stuart family photo" and it remained that way for months in my mind, a picture of my great-great-grandfather's family. But I'd begun looking at the image differently. Tempy, my great-great-grandmother, is in the center. Women fill most of the frame, three of them Black and biracial. It was time to do some renaming.

BACK HOME FROM GRANDMA'S FUNERAL, I DRAGGED MY SUIT-case up our bluestone path, slick from spring's damp breath. It was too cold for the third day of June or the strawberries growing along our walkway, small and obscured by all the weeds.

After my mother-in-law was back home in Croton and my girls were asleep, or pretending to be, I crept into my office. The wheels of my chair screeched across the wood floor as I turned on the heat and clicked on the computer in one motion. At the top of my inbox was an email response to my year-old post to RSmith, but it wasn't from Renee: *After quite a bit of research I believe I am also "Tempe's" Great Great Great Grand-daughter. My dad is the R. Smith (Robert Stuart Smith) on the post prior to yours. Have you found out anything more? Monique*

My grandmother
Lillie Mae Ford (née Daniel), c. 1950.

CHAPTER 7

UNITED DAUGHTERS

Monique's hair is sandy, eyes green, her skin like buttercream. We look nothing alike, but both of us are married to White men with whom we have two daughters each. We both live in New Jersey, just thirty miles between us. We are both obsessed with our family's history in a way our immediate families don't understand and view our coming together on the heels of my grandmother's death as a sign.

By our third email exchange, we were calling each other "cousin." Still, I approached her with the tenuous enthusiasm reserved for new sweethearts. I was scared that I might scare her away. She felt the same. "Please don't think I'm an ancestry.com stalker," she wrote after two weeks of online and phone exchanges, inviting my kids and me to visit.

She and her daughters were waiting for us in their driveway when we arrived, unbothered by the light rain. My girls bounded out of the car and ran to Monique's. They looked more like sisters than cousins and they weren't afraid. They hugged each other as though they were long-lost friends then filed into the house to play Barbies and Wii in the basement by the Colonel's sword. Amid the elation of being together in person for the first time, I almost forgot the intended purpose of the visit, Monique's big ancestral find. She and I followed our girls down.

Monique planned on getting a special box for it, but for now the Colonel's sword lay in the middle of the pool table in her basement. Just as soon as we arrived downstairs she unwrapped the sword from its thick gauzy blanket and I let out a mortified shriek. The Colonel's name was engraved on the blade next to etchings of a man and woman embracing and a bare-bottomed child clutching a woman's leg in front of a columned building. The handle grip was a man's face. His thick mustache bulged over his smile and under his closed eyes like he'd just tasted something good. He was wearing a helmet with a lion perched on top of it. A smiling man with a lion on his head? It reminded me of the picture of our ancestors, the Colonel grinning, surrounded by women who at any moment might have struck with a vengeance. Using the White archivist's gloves that Monique handed to me, I ran my hand along the sword over and over again, wondering how something so narrow and beautiful could be a threat to anyone.

Even though people called him Colonel, Stuart was listed as a private on his muster roll. He joined a Confederate Guards Regiment of the Louisiana Militia under Major General Mansfield Lovell in March of 1862. He served in this volunteer unit for a month, defending New Orleans, where he worked and lived, until Union Navy admiral David Farragut snuck up on the city from the Gulf and threatened to bombard it. The capture was a major turning point in the war and the end of the Colonel's military career. After that battle, he didn't do any more fighting. He gave money to the cause instead.

If Tempy had wanted to escape slavery, this was the time to do it. When federal forces took over New Orleans in May 1862, slaves began to flee their masters and seek refuge with the man in charge, Union general Benjamin Butler. He employed some of the self-emancipators who turned up at his camp but turned others away. "What would be the state of things if I allowed all the slaves from the plantations to quit their employ and come with the lines is not to be conceived by the imagination," he said.[1] He was more concerned with stoking Unionism among Whites than freeing enslaved Blacks. I doubt Butler would have found a place for Tempy, a woman in her forties who had a toddler in tow and may have also been pregnant. She would give birth to her daughter Violet the next year. A better bet would have been Butler's colleague General John Phelps. He welcomed anyone who could make it to Camp Parapet, about seven miles upriver from the city.

But that's the catch—would she have been able to make it? Would that have been too much for Tempy, with baby Alfred and another child on the way? In my first trimester of pregnancy with Desiree, it was near impossible for me to walk the half mile across Central Park, my constitutional. I was so nauseous that I had to sit down several times in the process. It got to feel a little dangerous, to be so vulnerable in the middle of the expanse that was normally my sanctuary, so I stopped taking this walk until the nausea stopped many months later. Maybe Tempy, who likely didn't know how to read or write, felt safer staying put.

From what we know, many enslaved women in New Orleans seem to have felt that way. Harriet Barrett, enslaved in New Orleans, was "most scared to death when de war end. Us still in New Orleans and all de shoutin' dat took place 'cause us free!" she said. "Massa say I's free as him, but iffen I wants to cook for him and missy I gits $2.50 de month," so that's what she did until she married.[2] "Women, in fact, had as much to fear of Union soldiers as they did of Confederates," writes Deborah Gray White in *Ar'n't I a Woman?: Female Slaves in the Plantation South*. Upon emancipation, Black women reported being raped by Union soldiers in camps and cabins from Virginia to Mississippi.

The Stuarts were the devil Tempy knew.

With reconstruction on the horizon, the future must have looked bright. The end of slavery, equal rights and citizenship, the vote for Black men were all on their way.

And things must have seemed especially promising in New Orleans. Its public schools opened to Black children, and the city's own Pinckney Benton Stewart Pinchback became the country's first Black governor (and the last until 1990). Mississippi elected Hiram Revels the first Black US senator in 1870, the same year Tempy moved to Ocean Springs to work there for the Colonel and Elizabeth.

MONIQUE BOUGHT THE SWORD ON EBAY AS A FATHER'S DAY gift for her dad. "It's the only time I ever saw him speechless," she said. She arranged for delivery just as Congress made a formal apology for slavery with the disclaimer that their sorry in no way supported or called for reparations.

The house smelled like freshly baked bread. On her kitchen table, Monique had spread out food I try to stay away from—chicken salad loaded with mayonnaise and a cheese plate. We settled at the kitchen table across from an enormous pedigree chart propped up in the picture bay window and Mo, as I had already begun calling her, cracked open a binder labeled "Dionne" in old-fashioned print on the spine.

"Tell me about Mississippi and New Orleans," she said, pen and notebook at the ready. Her family never visited, so I showed her pictures of mine, matching the faces with the names on the chart. I handed her a photo of Grandma Lillie Mae in a pastel hat in front of her old church with my brothers on Easter, and told Mo that my grandmother had known her great-grandmother, Tempy Elizabeth, and

Tempy Elizabeth's son Alf, the famous musical cousins. In a way, you might also say that I'd known Tempy Elizabeth's grandson, Monique's uncle JoJo Smith. He started a studio, JoJo's Dance Factory, that would morph into Broadway Dance in New York City, where I spent many Friday nights taking jazz classes with my college roommate. Dennis had taken classes there, too, before we met.

We talked about the significant age gap between Alf and Josephine that still had me questioning if they had been siblings or uncle and niece. We talked about our bodies, how they'd changed since having our daughters, how we were teased growing up about our skin and our hair. In her old neighborhood in Staten Island, mixed as the one where I grew up in South Jersey, she'd been called "Oreo" too.

"I thought I'd be too White for you," she told me.

Her hair was gathered in a small tight ponytail. Mine hung loose past my shoulders and puffed out, half processed, half natural. I was still debating what to do with it next. I'd been having that conversation with myself on and off since I was eight, freed my long hair from its pony for the first time, and was told by my older friend that I looked like a girl who was fast.

I'd gathered my fast-girl hair up in my fist that day and twisted it tight so it lay as flat on my head as possible, like Monique's. Our girls all had variations of curly hair, now frizzed from the weather. My oldest was just entering the maze of Black/mixed–girl hair trauma, forever wishing it were straight. Maybe they could walk together through it. Maybe we all could.

"I've been thinking of joining the Daughters of the Confederacy," I told her. Monique let out a whoop that made her chest shake.

It was not that I wanted to sit around with a bunch of women I'd never met glorifying people who fought to uphold slavery. The same way I doubt the people of color who first infiltrated all-White country clubs were just dying to eat club sandwiches and play a round of golf surrounded by people who did not want them there. It was not a matter of want. It was a matter of right, the right to belong, and of taking it.

I imagined meeting my new cousins, the Stuart family, at a reunion where the Colonel's lancet would be displayed for all of us to behold or touch or spit on as we saw fit. I imagined myself flying down to Mississippi for a local Daughters meeting, borrowed lancet in hand. I imagined them flagellating themselves for having kept their club closed to the fuller story of the Confederacy, to the darker faces spawned by Confederate men and enslaved women.

The application requirements on the Daughters website said that the Colonel's sword would not be proof enough. They wanted paper records, like a birth certificate. Imagine that: some official stamped document with Tempy and the Colonel's names under "parents." Even Grandma Lillie Mae, born Black and poor at the turn of the century, didn't have one of those, and had had to guess at her age. I didn't know how I'd be able to prove that I qualified, but it seemed important, like correcting an inaccuracy in a news article. I thought of Percival Everett's story "The Appropriation of

Cultures." The main character, a Black Southerner, drives around with a Confederate flag in the window of his truck, befuddling all the townspeople. By adopting the symbol, he takes control of it. That's what I wanted. Control. But I'd seen time and again how control did not translate into power. The election of a mixed-race man who identified as Black to the office of president did not make the country post-racial.

Days before I first visited Monique, Henry Louis Gates Jr., a Black professor at Harvard with two biracial daughters and the go-to scholar for all things African American genealogy, was arrested while trying to get into his house in Cambridge, Massachusetts. Even President Obama criticized the incident, then invited Gates and the officer who'd arrested him to the White House for a beer. Obama's critique caused the biggest single drop in his support among White voters. "When I saw Gates's picture on my computer, I thought he was dead," Monique said before she called the girls to come eat dessert. I knocked on wood and crossed myself. Gates's work had introduced me to the stories of once-enslaved African American women when I was in college, my first glimpse of what life might have been like for Tempy.

As I cleared the research from the table to make way for food, I glanced up at the family tree on the wall. There were the Colonel and Tempy at the top, Monique and me at the bottom, and dozens of names equaling almost two hundred years in between. Tempy died on March 1, 1925.

Exactly seventy-five years later, Desiree was born. Grandma Lillie Mae died and Monique arrived. All things bad and good happen in threes. But no one else was dying. Nothing was ending. Except perhaps for otherness, lonesomeness. In that house where I was not the only, only, only, we were just beginning.

My family gathered after a presentation at the Montclair History Center.

(back) Dad, Dennis, Mom, me, Granny Louise, my sister Debra, my sister Diana, Monique; (front) my grandniece, Selena; and my daughters, Devany and Desiree.

CHAPTER 8

THE PECAN AND HOW TO GROW IT

We'd had the where-babies-come-from talk, but I really didn't want to have to explain the whole forced-sex thing over pizza to my nine- and six-year-old.

"Why did we have slavery?" Dezi asked soon after our visit with our cousins. She wanted to know about Tempy, and why she would have agreed to work for her enslavers after the Civil War had already ended.

I speculated. "She probably couldn't read or write. She probably didn't know where to go." I didn't mention what most likely kept her there—her children with the Colonel.

"Mom, if we were back in those days and I met you, I would buy you so I could free you," Desiree said.

"If I met you, I'd free you and make you a queen," Devany added.

"You're both very kind," I said. Desiree had just started calling herself biracial and I didn't want to say anything to upend what seemed like a victory. I didn't tell her that back then she would have been considered Black. She would have been a slave too.

Before our pizza dinner, Monique had sent me a link to an orchard in Georgia that sold Stuart pecan trees.

"Ya know we'll be planting one on the property next spring, with a ceremony and all. LOL!" she wrote, but I didn't think she was joking.

Someone she'd met on a genealogy site had forwarded her newspaper articles about the Colonel's vast pecan farm in Ocean Springs and his generosity to the local Methodist church. This fellow "geni" thought we all might be connected through slavery. One of her husband's ancestors had taken piano lessons from Tempy Elizabeth. Like Monique and I, she was in an interracial marriage, and she had a research partner in her sister-in-law. I took in the details of the articles she sent about the Colonel. One, from the society pages of the *Baltimore Sun*, was titled "Marriage of a Mexican Editor in Maryland." The Colonel's niece, Tilly Handy, was the bride. "The wooing was done" at Stuart's country house in Ocean Springs, and it was there, against the backdrop of the Gulf, that the couple "formed a strong attachment for each other" and were engaged within a matter of days.

Then we found the Colonel's obituary in the *Daily Picayune*: "Death of a Distinguished Southerner."

Mississippi lost a most valued and energetic adopted citizen when the hand of death laid low the stalwart veteran, Col. W. R. Stuart, at his home Ocean Springs, on the 29th.

The obit said he'd moved to Ocean Springs from New Orleans in 1874, that he grafted soft-shell pecans and was elected as a member of one of Louisiana's constitutional conventions.[1] I wondered if it was the infamous one, the site of the New Orleans Massacre of 1866, where dozens of people were killed after protesting the Black codes.

The Colonel had important friends from New Orleans, including a bishop and another colonel, William Hill Howcott, who came to mourn him:

Colonel Stuart's obsequies were followed by the whole population of the town. Business was suspended, streets were closed, and great respect was shown to his memory. He left no children, the only member of his family surviving him is his invalid wife, who resides in Ocean Springs, their old home.

The newspaper, the record, obliterating the lives of six people in four words.

I still hadn't found anything besides a few census records that proved Josephine's existence, let alone her connection to the Colonel. I'd struck out twice with death certificate requests to the State of Mississippi for her and was waiting to hear on my third try. Even information about her minister husband seemed only to remain in Uncle Henry's memory. I called Saint James Methodist Church to see if they had any records on the Reverend James Ford, and a kind parishioner who doubled as the unofficial church secretary returned the call a month later.

"Unfortunately," she said, "there are very few records of the church's history and the ones we do have aren't very good." Meanwhile, the White Methodist church that had sent Mo pictures of stained-glass windows dedicated to the Colonel and his wife had its own history closet, two locations, and full-time paid staff.

In the newspaper articles we had, the Colonel was called "the father of the pecan industry in the South." He had developed a variety that was named after him, the Stuart pecan. That was the first thing my grandpa told me about his grandpa—that he was a pecan farmer. When I would think about what it was like for my dad growing up in that coastal town, I would picture him perched on a branch, swinging one leg, carefree, though I couldn't tell you what a pecan tree looked like or if its branches were tall and wide enough to hold a growing boy.

Monique found the Colonel's book, *The Pecan and How to Grow It*, online and bought the last copy. The pamphlet describes where pecans grow, the best ways to plant, how far apart to put the seedlings. It claims, basically, that pecans will save humanity. Inside is a picture of the Stuart pecans on exhibit at the 1893 World's Fair in Chicago. The Stuart Pecan Company published the book that same year, the text probably serving as much as an advertisement as an informational manual.

"When the wild Indian had this country all to himself and roamed through these vast forests, the Pecan tree furnished him a very reliable source from which to lay up a store of most excellent food. The White man has never paid much attention to the nut until within the last few years, and now they are proving themselves more worthy of cultivation each succeeding year on account of their superior excellence."

One reason why "the white man" started paying attention to pecan cultivation was the "Gulf Coast freeze." Freezing temperatures in the winters of 1886 and 1887 decimated citrus orchards along the Gulf of Mexico. The Colonel's orchards were undoubtedly among them.

Later in the book, the Colonel quotes an editorial from the New Orleans *Times-Democrat* that boasts that the income that's come in from his trees will be "a future endowment for his children and grandchildren, one that will pay better and is more sure than stocks or bonds or business enterprises of any kind, if ever so promising." That's an endowment this family has never seen.

Since "experience is the great teacher," the Colonel sent a letter to pecan growers around the country soliciting their insights on best pecan-growing practices and reproduced it and their responses in his book. Missing from these pages is, conspicuously, the true father of pecan culture—and commercial pecan production. His name was Antoine and he was the enslaved gardener at Oak Alley Plantation in Vacherie, Louisiana. In 1846, Antoine successfully propagated a pecan tree, making history. His technique made widespread commercial production of the nut possible. Thirty years later, his pecan won the "best pecan exhibited" at the Philadelphia Centennial Exhibition, the first world's fair held in the United States.

The Colonel's pecan exhibit was one of tens of thousands at the Columbian Exposition, the world's fair marking the four-hundred-year anniversary of Columbus landing in the Americas, with American innovation as its theme. The Colonel may have taken a ride on the world's first Ferris wheel or sampled the world's first instant-mix pancakes, served by Nancy Green, the formerly enslaved woman whom the world would come to know as Aunt Jemima. Maybe he passed the young writer Paul Laurence Dunbar, whose multiple jobs included cleaning one of the big domes. Maybe he heard Frances Ellen Watkins Harper proclaim, "If the fifteenth century discovered America to the Old World, the nineteenth is discovering woman to herself," in an address to the World's Congress of Representative Women. "Today, there are red-handed men in our republic," Harper said, "who walk unwhipped of justice, who richly deserve to exchange the ballot of the freeman for the wristlets of the felon." If the Colonel ventured into the Haiti Pavilion to hear Frederick Douglass speak, Ida B. Wells might have handed him her pamphlet: *The Reason Why the Colored American Is Not in the World's Columbian Exposition.*

"The exhibit of the progress made by a race in 25 years of freedom as against 250 years of slavery, would have been the greatest tribute to the greatness and progressiveness of American institutions which could have been shown the world," Wells writes in her introduction, which was reprinted in French and German so that foreign visitors wouldn't miss anything. She handed out ten thousand copies. "The wealth created by their industry has afforded to the white people of this country the leisure essential to their great progress in education, art, science, industry and invention." Wells's pamphlet criticized the fair for excluding African Americans and casting them negatively, in what she described as "a clear, plain statement of facts concerning the oppression put upon the colored people in this land of the free and home of the brave."

Black people could work at and buy a ticket to enter the fair, but their contributions to industry weren't on display at the main fairground, which was nicknamed "the White City" and highlighted European inventions. For a glimpse of "primitive" lifestyles, guidebooks suggested visiting the Midway fairground, where there was a replica of a Dahomey village complete with huts and Black people beating tom-toms. After extensive protests and negotiations, fair officials offered up a special day for African American visitors, but Wells considered "Negro Day" superficial.

The University of Georgia's agricultural college describes the Stuart pecan as the most widely known and planted cultivar in the Southeast, a standard to measure others against. What began as a hobby became a second career for the Colonel, one that was possible after he'd made a fortune cultivating and selling sugar with slave labor.

I knew I could not grow a Stuart pecan tree in my yard. I didn't have the skill, or the will. But I had a farm ship the fruit to me. Tempy would have baked pies and maybe bread and other sweet treats with them. She would have known the difference between a Stuart pecan and any other. As Tiya Miles writes in *All That She Carried,* "Wild pecans sustained Indigenous Americans for millennia and African Americans for generations."

I can't cook fancy, but I know a bit about what food to eat depending on my need. A sprinkle of cinnamon can help curb a caffeine craving. Fresh turmeric root added to any meal reduces inflammation; ground turmeric swallowed straight works well too. Kale, fish oils, and blueberries are good antidotes to depression. Food is love, even when, or maybe especially when, it's simple, like Nikkie's steamed crawfish or the sliced apples my sponsor Erik fanned out on a plate next to his quartered sandwich, in an act of self care, at the artist's colony where we met.

When I was little, if you weren't watching me, I'd eat an entire jar of pickle spears. I'd eat until my belly churned. I'd start with the thin line of seeds marching up the center, remnants of what the plants used to be, salty like the ocean and ferment, slippery like birth. I saw my grandmother drink some of the murky green juice once. She was probably making potato salad. My mother showed me how to dice the spears. Then she'd dump them into her potatoes followed by a splash of the juice, one of three of her secret ingredients. But my potato salad never comes out right. It's always too mushy. For Thanksgiving, instead, I decided that I would bake a pecan pie with my great-great-grandfather's nuts, as my great-great-grandmother must have done.

His sword was now lying on our dining room table in its cotton sheath with a pair of archivist gloves, so no one would dare try to pick it up bare-handed. My father came to see it. He'd barely said anything about his family's picture that I'd found on the internet, but the sword grabbed his attention immediately. I thought he'd be disappointed when I explained that it wasn't a part of the Colonel's military dress, like I'd originally imagined, but instead a part of his Knights of Pythias uniform. A fraternal order similar to the Masons, the Knights of Pythias was organized in 1864 to renew brotherly spirit in the wake of the Civil War. My father turned the blade to the light so he could see the Colonel's inscription and told me something I'd never known before: he, my dad, had also belonged to a fraternal order. He must have taken the secret society thing pretty seriously. He'd joined the Prince Hall Masons while we were living in Maine. Prince Hall was a leader in the free Black community in Boston and a Revolutionary War hero who fought against slavery and for the education and full citizenship of Black people. Scholars believe he penned Belinda Royall's petition for reparations, the first in the country. When the White Masonic lodge in Boston wouldn't let him and other Black men join, Hall joined an Irish lodge instead.

Eventually he received permission to start his own lodge, African Masonic Lodge, the first Black Freemason lodge in America.

For the week that the sword was in my care, I tried to meditate with it. An instrument of war converted into one of peace and reconciliation seemed appropriate for that space. My neighbors and my research were getting to me. (My neighbors were mad that we were subdividing our property. I was mad that I had to spend so much time with the Colonel to find out anything about Tempy.) I followed the guided meditation I'd learned when I was pregnant with Dezi, envisioning roots growing from my sacrum down through all the levels of the earth to its red-hot core. With every breath, I sucked up the earth's energy until it filled me. When I am really grounded, I can feel energy moving through me. When I am really agitated, I picture the energy radiating out through every person in the world. I start with all the people I love. I save my enemies for last. Cross-legged at the altar in my living room, my fingers on the metal, I felt nothing, not even anger at the Colonel for enslaving Tempy, for not ever acknowledging Josephine as his daughter. He was a cipher and I felt empty.

CHAPTER 9
THE FIRE THIS TIME

Grandma's house burned down this weekend."

My cousin Nikkie spoke into the phone evenly, her voice sweet, like it's always been. Her father, my uncle Henry, had been inside. He suffered burns bad enough to put him in the hospital until the new year.

It was mid-December. I was waiting for the Stuart Papers to arrive, doing the Christmas and Kwanzaa shopping, and preparing for a women's-only solstice celebration. It was afternoon when the phone rang, the sun weak and hiding. Nikkie had been driving back and forth between her temporary home in Mississippi and the hospital in Baton Rouge, a ten-hour round trip, and I could hear her fatigue. At first, Henry was taken to Tulane Medical Center in New

Orleans, but there weren't enough resources for his care, my cousin said, so he was moved to Baton Rouge General's burn center. In between visits, Nikkie tried to find a place for him to convalesce once he was released; a diabetic in jeopardy of losing his leg, Henry would need some kind of assisted living. He'd been trying to repair the damage from Katrina while living in the house, but a lack of financial help from the government and his poor health meant that things had been going slowly. The gas heaters he was using to keep warm or the hot plates for cooking had probably started the fire.

My favorite uncle, our family griot, the youngest of five, like me.

Nikkie grew up a few miles from our grandparents and had more time with them than I did. She has rich dark skin like her mother and, once, when she was walking with Grandpa toward his apartment in a mostly Black neighborhood, a lady asked her if "that White man" was bothering her. She told the woman that the White man was her grandpa. She couldn't have been more than ten. He was babysitting.

On that same phone call, my conversation with Nikkie turned to the past. Grandpa's mother, Josephine, worked for a White doctor "and the doctor was fond of her," she told me. "At some point they got together and Grandpa was the product." Our grandmother, Lillie Mae, had told Nikkie this story and that the doctor's name was Stuart. There was a Dr. H. L. Stewart, a White man, in Ocean Springs in 1905, the year Grandpa was born. But his title was probably just an honorific, since on the 1900 census he's listed as a nurs-eryman. A more likely candidate is Dr. R. A. Switzer, born in 1876, a year after Josephine. He was the son of the Colonel and Elizabeth's neighbor, a photographer who likely took the Stuart/Burton family photo. In 1900, the younger Switzer bought his father's property, and he got his license to practice medicine two years later.[1] This would explain why Grandpa was so very White-looking in comparison to his siblings. Or it could be a case of the recessive becoming dominant. Genes sometimes rebel too.

She could have had an affair. She could have been sexu-ally assaulted. This was the first time I'd heard the story, and I still don't know if it's true. Earlier in my life, speculation about her and the doctor might have closed my heart to Josephine. Now I wasn't interested in judging her sexuality. And I didn't want to know whether this doctor was a Stuart relative, or if my grandfather was the product of incest; it was too close to my own wound. The suggestion made me think of her differently, not just as somebody's child, or somebody's mother, but as a sexual being, a person who might have had an unconventional sex life or suffered from sexual trauma, as I had.

Josephine was nineteen when she became a mother. James was in his early thirties. She would sometimes make Grandpa wear a dress when he got into trouble, Nikkie said. It was supposed to deter him from playing baseball while he was punished, but it didn't work. He still played, dress and all.

Nikkie had two decorative glasses that she'd taken out of the house on Conti for safer keeping as soon as she heard Katrina was coming. The glasses were a deep shade of wine red with ridged tops, one a tumbler and the other a chalice without a stem. They looked regal in the pictures Nikkie texted, even though they stood only a few inches tall. The chalice was inscribed with the name "Tempy Burton." The tumbler, "Josie Ford." Family heirlooms. Things our grandmothers had touched. Tangible proof of Josephine.

Both glasses bore the name "Mount Clemens" and a date, August 1905. Josie would have been very pregnant with my grandpa, who was born in October of that year. The decision to travel to Mount Clemens in her final trimester might have been precautionary. Yellow fever had killed more than forty-one thousand people in New Orleans alone since the early nineteenth century and was still a problem then in the Mississippi Gulf region where she and her mother lived. In June of that year, New Orleans declared a state of emergency when one hundred people came down with the disease. By August, the city had asked for federal help. President Theodore Roosevelt assigned a US surgeon general to the public health campaign. New Orleans was fumigated, screens were placed over cisterns to keep out mosquitoes, and other breeding grounds for the insects were destroyed. Residents who didn't comply with the measures were fined. By October, the epidemic was over, and the country would never see another yellow fever outbreak again. Tempy and Josephine's mother-daughter trip before the birth of my grandfather would have taken them from one watery town to another. Nicknamed "Bath City," Mount Clemens, Michigan, was known for the mineral "black water" that bubbled below the town, thought to be rich with healing properties. After the first bathhouse was built there in 1873, people flocked to the city from around the country for a series of fifty-cent baths said to combat all kind of ailments, from gout and diabetes to hysteria and alcoholism. By 1899, Mount Clemens had seven bathhouses catering to a varied clientele. The Park Hotel attracted elite guests like Tammany Hall boss Charles Murphy and President Teddy Roosevelt's daughter Alice, while Saint Joseph Sanitarium and Bathhouse was for the everyman. The sanitarium's third floor was used as a fifty-bed hospital, and Saint Joseph proudly claimed that it was open to anyone regardless of race so long as the bath seeker came with a prescription from a doctor.

The other bathhouses in Mount Clemens in 1905 were not so open-minded. The town's segregation policy wasn't openly advertised. But an August 25, 1905, article in the *Mount Clemens Monitor* documented the town practice plainly: "A young colored man, university graduate, left Mt. Clemens yesterday because he could not get the baths." It would be fifteen years before Henry Lightbourne opened the Mount Clemens Hotel and Mineral Baths for Colored Guests.[2]

Maybe Tempy and Josephine had kept the glasses from their trip under lock and key like Grandma Lillie Mae did and only brought them out on special occasions. Maybe Great-Grandma Josie drank from her glass every night with dinner to be reminded of the mother-daughter voyage, or maybe she took a ceremonial sip from it just once a year on her birthday or to mark the new year. Maybe she only used it when she was drinking spirits or calling them, pouring a few drops into her houseplants or outside in the garden.

Tempy's chalice would make a lovely Kikombe cha Umoja—the Unity Cup used for drinking and pouring libations to thank and remember our African ancestors. I first learned about Kwanzaa while browsing in a Black-owned bookstore in New Brunswick, on assignment for the *Home News*. My daughters first learned about it in religious education class. The Unitarian Universalist Association was an early supporter of Kwanzaa, and every year our congregation features the celebration in its holiday pageant. Our family celebrated it for the first time the Christmas after I found the family photo because my daughters, then five and eight, begged me to. The gold-embroidered tunics that Dennis's sister had bought for them in Morocco were too big then. On the heels of the fire, celebrating Kwanzaa for the third time, the tunics finally fit.

"Is Tempy really her name?" Devany wanted to know, since the Kwanzaa book we read from said our ancestors' African names were lost. Kwanzaa's second principle is Kujichagulia, or self-determination, and always made me think of the names we're given and the names we claim. According to census reports, Tempy was born in Louisiana, Alabama, or North Carolina, not Africa. I don't know who

gave Tempy her name—her parents or the people who enslaved her. Tempy is most likely short for Temperance, a
popular name at that time. Shortly after she was born, as
American Temperance Societies formed around the country, the name would become synonymous with abstinence
from drinking.

*My cousin Nikkie and me with the glasses that
belonged to Tempy and Josephine.*

CHAPTER 10

SPIRITS

Quiet as it's kept, I am not supposed to talk about Alcoholics Anonymous or incest, two of the most significant features of my life. Anonymity is the spiritual foundation of AA, its twelfth tradition states, and the tradition before that recommends that AAs always maintain personal anonymity when it comes to the press, radio, television, and film.

But the ways in which AAs practice these principles vary widely. The only step we all take in the same way is the first one: we don't drink. (Or fill in the blank; AA's twelve steps have been applied to countless other addictions from drugs to food to sex.) The next eleven steps and the twelve traditions are personally and individually expressed. We take what we like and leave the rest. That's how I can break the eleventh tradition, of maintaining anonymity at the level of the press, and practice the twelfth step, of carrying the message to other alcoholics, in the same sentence. That's how I can allow myself to remain in a program created by and for White Christian men.

The first AA meeting that I went to for myself, as opposed to for my boyfriend or for my college counselors, was in a dark YMCA basement not far from my college campus. I could not have had less in common with the speaker, a White guy who'd barely graduated high school and was addicted to heroin. But when he talked about how he felt, so separate and ill at ease in his body, how that feeling had been subsiding since he started coming to AA, I knew I was in the right place. The emotions, and not the package they came in, spoke to me.

That speaker became part of a crew of young people I got sober with in New York City in 1991. The identification that I found with them, mixed with desperation, kept me returning. I'd already tried to kill myself and had been arrested twice for alcohol-related reasons. I was afraid that if these meetings didn't help me, I would end up in an insane asylum or dead.

I counted my days in meetings and in my journal at home and did what the sober people told me to:

Day 20. Lunch with Gerald and Lou. They're hysterical.

Day 21. Went to a sober birthday party with Meghan #3. Lou, Gerald, Kara, Eric and my sponsor were there!

Day 29. Had lunch with Lou, Gerald, and the Meghans. Bent Lou's and Gerald's ears about this guy, another actor, 13th-stepping me. They say that guy's in trouble.

On day fifty-one, I shared in a meeting the memories of sexual abuse that I feared would make me drink again. Afterward, six women approached me and gave me their phone numbers. Lou stuck around while I collected those numbers, then, during the long lull until my next class, stayed with me in the shadow of budding forsythia bushes and cherry trees in Central Park, making me laugh. Lou had been sober twelve months and was a year older than me, around twenty-three. He wasn't yet famous—he'd go on to win an Academy Award—but he was like a god to me then. How did anyone stay sober a whole year? That night, I stapled those phone numbers to my diary along with a gratitude list, something my sponsor had asked me to write up every day to help me change my attitude. The eighth thing I was grateful for was the time with Lou in Central Park, spring blooming all around us. The first thing was those six numbers, those women.

A woman old enough to be my mother became one of my closest friends. Our sobriety and not our biological ages was the glue. She was new to AA like me, Black, and incredibly beautiful. We both grew up in rural Northern towns, and we both felt a deep disconnect from our families but for different reasons—me because of the incest and my dad's drinking, her because she'd been adopted. At my bridal shower, my wedding, my baby shower, and an outdoor concert where guys tried to pick us up when they should have been listening to Chaka Khan crooning "I Feel for You," everyone thought we were sisters. We were. We are.

It was a sober sister who told me about some other sober sisters who were looking for a new roommate when I needed a new place to stay. It was a sober sister who told me about the newspaper where her husband worked that was hiring, the newspaper where I ended up getting my first professional journalism award. It was sober sisterhood that drove me to give my number to a newcomer, a Black girl who'd lived in my dorm freshman year, even though she'd always been low-key terrible to me. When she called, the first thing she did was apologize. "You were pretty and middle-class and there wasn't enough room for two of us," meaning two pretty, middle-class Black girls in our mostly White campus and dorm. She verbalized a fear that had bobbed around in my mind for so long, like a ship with no port: that there wasn't enough room for us, that we couldn't have more than one story. We began to talk regularly. We grew up together and grew each other up. And our sacred space, our saving grace, was the women's meetings.

My sponsor took me to my first women's AA meeting when I was still counting days. It was in a sleek skyscraper in midtown Manhattan owned by a publishing company. We read the eleventh step from the Big Book that begins, "Upon awakening, we consider the day ahead," and then recommends, "Be quick to see where religious people are right." I so appreciated that "where," the difference between "where" and "that." Then, for five minutes, we sat together in silence. I don't know if there is anything more humbling than that silence, except for maybe the next thing that happened: women started to share how they prayed and meditated. Each one had her own way. Lawyers, students, artists, atheists, teachers, Buddhists, mothers, daughters, gay, straight, all shared how they stayed connected and awake. They prayed and meditated in bathrooms, board-rooms, courtrooms, and at crosswalks, waiting for the light to change. They prayed to higher powers that were trees, Virgin Mothers, or Our Fathers. One woman's higher power was the color blue because she could see it every-where, even on the subway.

After that, mixed meetings became the fat in my diet. The women's meetings were all the nutrients. But in both cases, some of the people were hard to stomach.

After a women's meeting at a temple in my hometown, an older sober woman told me not to share any more about having been molested. Everybody else told me not to listen to her. Another sober sister, an incest survivor, offered to host a meeting at her house for sober sexual abuse survivors, because there were just so many of us and we needed to talk about both things. (According to the *American Journal on Addictions*, 75 percent of women who enter substance abuse treatment programs report having experienced sexual abuse. Another study in the *Journal of Traumatic Stress* indicated that 90 percent of women who became dependent on alcohol were violently abused by a parent or were sexually traumatized as a child.) When I announced this new women survivors' meeting during the break at a mixed meeting, a man pulled me aside to tell me that I shouldn't, that it wasn't AA. Sexual abuse, he said, was an outside issue.

"AA has no opinion on outside issues," according to its tenth tradition. Alcoholics Anonymous had learned from the organizations that came before it, like the Washingtonians. When the Washingtonian movement was founded, on an April day in 1840 in Baltimore, Maryland, its members had one goal: to stop drinking in order to improve their lives. But as the movement gained in popularity, swelling to half a million people, they allowed anyone to drop in no matter their purpose—from Walt Whitman to Abraham Lincoln, who delivered a campaign speech. Some members promoted causes like Prohibition and the abolition of slavery. Within a decade, the movement had collapsed.

I spent the first decade of my sobriety hating that dude and certain he was wrong. I spent the next decade thinking he was right. Now, in my third decade, I think it doesn't matter. I'm sure talk of incest made folks squeamish. It makes me squeamish to hear about it. But it's what happened to me and it's what I drank over and talking about it is what I needed to do. For the first time ever, I put my need over someone else's comfort, and over the traditions of AA, unabashedly, unapologetically. I consider sexual abuse survivorship a protected affinity status. And I knew that talking about it was a matter of life or death for me. AA was a perfectly imperfect place full of perfectly imperfect people, like my family, like my country, and I could take what I liked and leave the rest without having to leave.

My dad had gone to meetings as well, but after a few months he opted out of AA and turned to our church instead. He joined his friend Tank in ministering to men living at a local shelter and battling addiction by studying the Bible with them. I still have the *Big Book* Dad gave me when I was counting days and told him I was going to meetings. "There are some nice people there," he said, handing the heavy blue tome, AA's bible, over to me. "It really helps some people." But it did not help him.

One of my sponsees left AA for church as well. She was around my age, new, Black, and I was excited to work together. I met her at the women's eleventh-step meeting in New York City, which didn't have many Black members. After a few weeks of chatting on the phone and beginning to delve into the *Big Book*, she announced that she didn't want to go to any more AA meetings. She was going to get sober through her church. But she still wanted to call me; she needed someone to listen to her and tell her what to do. Twelve-step sobriety doesn't work like that. It isn't something you can give. It's a circle of mutual aid that the book *A Woman's Way Through the Twelve Steps* describes as a feminine model of support and healing. If I'd had "the answers" I would have typed them up or bottled them and sold them. Better than that, I would have stayed home and just lived them. I was sober proof that AA worked, but my sponsee did not want to have to deal with the crappy parts of the program that made her uncomfortable— sitting in meetings with so many White people, consuming antiquated, patriarchal language in books written by and for straight White men. I understood her. I was her. Hell is other people and other people are necessary for healing. It just is how it is.

"Almost without exception, alcoholics are tortured by loneliness," the *Twelve Steps and Twelve Traditions* maintains. "Even before our drinking got bad and people cut us off, nearly all of us suffered the feeling we didn't quite belong." For underrepresented people, the loneliness is only compounded.

It's why I joined the National Association of Black Journalists, then Mocha Moms, a national organization that supports women of color raising children, and the Black Lives of Unitarian Universalism. It is a rarity for me to be in exclusively Black spaces. I would not entirely realize this until the coronavirus pandemic, when I began going to twelve-step meetings online and was invited to speak at one for Black people. In the decades of my recovery, I'd been to women's meetings and young people's meetings but never to a meeting for Black people exclusively. When the leader made the announcement, "If you are a person who does not identify as BIPOC, please send me a message in the chat and I will help you find a different meeting," I wanted to cheer and weep for how much I'd needed permission to gather in affinity.

In a letter to the cofounder of Alcoholics Anonymous, psychiatrist Carl Jung wrote of the craving for alcohol as a "spiritual thirst of our being for wholeness." "Alcohol in Latin is 'spiritus' and you use the same word for the highest religious experience as well as for the most depraving poison. The helpful formula therefore is: spiritus contra spirit."[1] The Spirit against spirits. The Spirit to fight spirits.

Spiritual versus religious. Too religious, not religious enough. The God question is fraught for many who come to AA in desperation but struggle with the program's religious undertones. The evangelical Christian Oxford Group heavily influenced AA. By the end of the 1930s, the two parted ways when AA wanted to focus solely on drinking and the Oxford Group wanted to focus on Christ.

When I was around twelve years sober, I was at one of my regular meetings when something especially religious was read as a discussion topic from a book written by an AA who started out in the Oxford Group. The tone of the reading gave me a sinking feeling. It wasn't the first time that I felt worse after reading from it, like I was in trouble and headed for hell. The book was popular and has sold close to ten million copies since it was first published in the late 1940s. But it did not reflect the God of my understanding, the God I had worked to build a relationship with for over a decade. As much as I loved Jesus Christ, and the comfort he surely brought to generations of my ancestors during and after slavery, it was his life as a man that I celebrated. Sitting in that meeting that I did not want to return to, I knew that I wanted to follow Christ's example, not worship him. I could no longer pretend that I was a Christian.

CHAPTER 11
HERETIC

Unitarianism is just slightly more popular today than witchcraft was in puritanical New England. Only 0.3 percent of Americans are Unitarian Universalists, and of those 5 percent are Black. That makes me a minority within a minority. Statements of faith rather than creeds, the wisdom of poetry rather than doctrine, children dedicated rather than cleansed of sin: this is what attracted me. At our daughters' dedication ceremony, we were instructed through the words of poet Kahlil Gibran: "You may give them your love but not your thoughts. . . . You may strive to be like them but seek not to make them like you." It's likely what drew many a Black UU before me, too, from Frances Ellen Watkins Harper to the psychologists Drs. Kenneth and Mamie Clark, whose doll test was used in *Brown v. Board of Education* to demonstrate the depths and pervasiveness of White supremacy. Maybe it's what attracted my great-great-great-grandfather also.

> After having been inclined to Unitarianism because it appeared to me less mysterious, I returned heartily to Trinitarianism as really the less mysterious of the two; and as the more scriptural. And now, Trinitarian thoroughly, I do not believe that our salvation depends upon our belief of these obtuse points, but upon our true conversion and obedience to God.[1]

Philadelphia minister A. Webster wrote this in a letter to William R. Stuart, the Colonel's father. It is one of over six hundred letters, poems, obituaries, and other mementos in the Stuart Papers. In these papers, the elder Stuart—Big Will, as I call him—copied down texts that struck him, saved keepsakes like his son Charles's certificate as a member of the Washingtonian Temperance Society, and pondered God on the page. As Big Will and Webster wrote back and forth about it over several years, Unitarianism was gaining prominence. The UU church in New Orleans, nicknamed the Strangers' Church, recorded baptisms of enslaved people. UU minister Theodore Parker's fiery speeches, during which he described democracy "of all the people, by all the people, for all the people," would influence Abraham Lincoln, and another, in which he wrote, "I do not pretend to understand the moral universe; the arc is a long one, my eye reaches but little ways," would inspire Martin Luther King Jr.

Big Will corresponded with his sons, friends, and colleagues on everything from slavery to professional setbacks—in his case, being sacked from his job as president of the Maryland State Senate. Someone related to Big Will's daughter, Susan, had been the keeper of this enormous commonplace book before loaning it for microfilming to the Mississippi State University Library. I'd ordered the Stuart Papers sure that I would find correspondence about Tempy and her family or maybe photocopied pages of a family bible with the names and births of slaves recorded. So strong was my faith that when I heard the UPS man's feet thunder up our stairs, I shouted to the kids, "Our family's history is here," and we all cheered. But there was nothing among the saved newspaper clippings or crosshatched letters about my enslaved relatives. Instead, the things that my third great-grandfather kept reflected the Stuarts' legacy in me: drinking, then quitting, and searching for God. Heresy, from the Greek "to choose." Big Will was a heretic like me.

In one letter to the Colonel written in the 1830s, Big Will wrote from Baltimore:

> My Dear Son,
>
> Continue at merchandise, be it your determination to give yourself no concern about any other occupation. When you have money to invest, purchase land, not with a view of cultivating, no never, never entangle yourself with the perplexity of slaves; if you do, you will repent it all your days.

This advice made me hope that his political opinions opposed slavery too. But what Big Will wrote and how he lived were two different things. He was very close friends with Edward Lloyd, whose family was among the largest property owners in terms of both land and slaves on Maryland's eastern shore. Frederick Douglass grew up on one of Lloyd's plantations and wrote about his harsh treatment there in his autobiography. In preparation for a US Senate run in 1824, Lloyd petitioned my great-great-great-grandfather for support; at the time, Big Will was the State Senate president.

"Should I go to Annapolis and the contest be between you and Col. Emory for the M.S. Senate," Big Will wrote to Lloyd that year, "I could not vote for either, that I was a friend to you both and hesitated not to avow it."

And later: "Shortly, in a day after you last came to hand, we met with a heavy loss, as well as a distressing one; two of our black boys, one about 21 the other about 19 years of age were drowned in Corsica Creek. They were worth as much as any servants in the county. I hope they are better off."

Stuart closed the letter "your unfortunate friend," and I couldn't tell if he was upset to be caught in the middle of his two friends or about the drowned enslaved young men.

In the end, it was a different friend who opposed Lloyd in the Senate: Ezekiel Chambers. Chambers and Big Will grew up together, and were among Washington College's earliest graduates. When Big Will was president of the Maryland Senate, he sent a letter to his equal in New Jersey introducing Chambers, newly deputized to confer with the legislatures of New Jersey, Delaware, and Pennsylvania on ways to prevent the absconding of Maryland's slaves to these nearby free states. (New Jersey was the only Northern state to support the 1850 Fugitive Slave Act.)

I carefully read through all of these documents late into the winter evenings hoping to find something that would explain Big Will's double-sided thinking, that would reconcile his deep love of God with his disregard for the enslaved. I found nothing.

Days before he died, he wrote to the Colonel, then living in Baton Rouge:

> *New Orleans, August 16, 1853*
>
> My Dear William,
>
> I have been distressed in not hearing from you, hope however your health is preserved, and that of all our relatives and friends is maintained? Our city continues to labour under the affecting? Malady. . . . The almighty knows what is best for all of his creatures . . . our duty is to pray to him. . . . Thank God we are all well. . . .
>
> Your affectionate father,
>
> Wm R. Stuart

But they were not all well. Five days later, the Colonel's brother wrote:

> My Dear William,
>
> Alas we have no more a father. . . . He breathed his last sigh like an infant. . . . I held his right hand in

mine and my left upon his heart. . . . And only a
few moments before he expired he asked and
called for you.

In the following weeks, the Colonel's brother Alexander
would write another twenty-plus dispatches to the Colonel
from his home on Dauphin Street, a litany of illness and
grief. His wife, Matilda, was okay but at least two of their
children were sick. William was getting better, the letters reported, but Peter was dreadfully ill. A month later, Alexander
would die just like his father in one of New Orleans's worst
yellow-fever epidemics. His funeral would be held at the
home where he'd written all those death-vigil letters, and
someone else would have to write to the Colonel that he
had no more a brother.

Big Will's death prompted reactions in both religious
and political spheres. "I can now see him, as at a Plantation
Appointment, he enjoyed worship with the negroes, his
countenance happy, looking up, his hand upon his heart,
and the tears streaming down his cheeks," J. C. Keener,
bishop of the Methodist Episcopal Church and editor of
the New Orleans *Christian Advocate*, wrote on the death of
his friend. Ezekiel Chambers's two-column eulogy in the
February 6 *Baltimore Patriot* covered everything from Big
Will's ascendance to president of the Maryland State Senate
to his father's service in the Revolutionary War and, finally,
Big Will's "reverse of fortune, not unusual to men who have
more distinguished themselves by their generous and liberal kindness, than by a disposition to accumulate wealth."

When Big Will was twenty-two, he became the first and only member of his family to join the Methodist Episcopal Church when he and his wife were converted at a camp meeting. In 1830, when some members split with the ME to form the Methodist Protestant Church, Big Will was called upon to preside at its initial convention in Baltimore.

He then passed on his religion to the Colonel, who financially supported his Methodist church in Ocean Springs and was known to host ministers in his home. Newspaper articles hailed the Colonel and his wife as God-fearing and described Elizabeth's "patient, gentle submission to God's will through all these years of trial [as having] preached sermons to many." Sister Stuart, as the writer called her, was bedridden for over twenty-seven years, but had been making a slow recovery over the past half dozen with the help of her nurse—Tempy.

Tempy's 1925 funeral was attended by three ministers, and her death was covered in at least two newspapers. Nothing in them told me what her hobbies were, how she felt about the state of the democracy, if she took a daily walk to the beach—the type of detail I tried to include when I wrote newspaper obituaries. Her funeral was held on a Monday afternoon and "was largely attended by both white and colored friends." Repeatedly referring to my great-great-grandmother as "Aunt Tempy," the papers mostly talk about her connection to the Stuarts. One of her obituaries ends with the detail that Elizabeth died two months before Tempy did. Even her death centered on the Stuarts.

TEMPY, JOSEPHINE, MY GRANDFATHER, AND MY FATHER WERE all raised Methodist and I attended a Methodist church too. Our religion, then, was an inheritance from both the enslaved and enslaving sides of our family.

John Wesley and his brother Charles tried to bring Methodism to the colony of Georgia in the 1730s, but it didn't really take, and they returned to England. Later, immigrants to the United States had more success. In 1766, an Irish immigrant named Barbara Heck began the first Methodist Society in New York City with her cousin Philip Embury. Betty, a woman Heck enslaved, was also a member of the group. Around 1808, an enslaved woman known as Old Elizabeth organized a Black women's prayer meeting in Baltimore, serving as its unofficial preacher. Enslaved women were among the first Methodists in America.

Wesley opposed slavery, and many early Methodist clergymen followed suit. Some preached openly against slaveholding and others actively sought Black converts, scholar Cynthia Lynn Lyerly writes in her contribution to *Discovering the Women in Slavery*. In the early years of the country, Methodism "was a major force in manumissions." The first Methodist Episcopal gathering, the Christmas Conference, held at Lovely Lane Chapel in Baltimore in 1784, proclaimed: "We view [slavery] as contrary to the Golden Law of God." It's likely that Richard Allen was ordained at this same conference. Allen was born into slavery, taught himself to read and write, and when he was seventeen bought his own freedom. After he and other Black congregants refused to move to the back of their Philadelphia church in what has been described as the first peaceful civil rights protest, Allen formed the African Methodist Episcopal Church in 1816. Mother Bethel in Philadelphia was the first AME church in the country.

In 1777, when the United States was in its infancy and she was just eleven, Old Elizabeth was separated from her mother by slavery. "At parting, my mother told me that I had 'nobody in the wide world to look to but God.' These words fell upon my heart with ponderous weight, and seemed to add to my grief," Old Elizabeth testified, adding that, after some time, "I betook myself to prayer, and in every lonely place I found an altar."

Through camp meetings, Bible classes, and love feasts, women enslaved in different locations could meet one another, forming sisterhoods and "fictive kin." As Lyerly writes, "Slave women lived not only with slavery's routine restraints upon their will; they also had to fight for control over their bodies" as frequent victims of sexual abuse. Under these circumstances, "spiritual possession takes on added significance." Possession, beyond demonstrating an enslaved woman's connection to God, "was by nature beyond the control of slave owners, and in this subtle way, slave women could reclaim some control over their bodies." The Methodist Episcopal Church's antislavery views did not guarantee equal treatment to Black people, enslaved or free, and by the 1830s strong antislavery sentiments had given way to complacency and silence in much of the Methodist Episcopal Church; a decade later, the ME would split into North and South over slavery. Regardless, Lyerly notes, "the experience of early Methodist slave women suggests that many bondwomen found in religion a means to resist internalizing whites' negative images of black women."

I had assumed that the Stuarts indoctrinated Tempy into Methodism. But she might have inherited her religion from her mother or the Methodist sisterhood, and not her enslavers. She could have had a church community while enslaved in New Orleans at Saint James AME. Just like Richard Allen's church in Philadelphia, Saint James split from the White Saint Paul's in 1848 when the church ruled that all Black members had to sit in the balcony. Free Black women fundraised to build Saint James (they advertised in the *Times-Picayune* in 1854 and 1856 to pay for building debt) and all the congregants helped with construction. Women carried bricks in their aprons. Some of their members fought for the Union. One famous congregant, Pinckney Benton Stewart Pinchback, would go on to become the first Black governor in the United States.

After the Civil War, the ME church formed a freedmen's aid society to help educate Black children and the formerly enslaved. My dad's alma mater, Gilbert Academy, was one of the schools under the ME's auspices. The North and South sections and earlier factions of the church had reunited to form the United Methodist Church by the late 1960s. But the African Methodist Episcopal Church would remain under its own authority.

I made the mistake once of calling Grandma Lillie Mae an African Methodist Episcopal, since that's what we were, forgetting that my dad had started off as a Methodist. She immediately set me straight. "I'm no AME," she said with a huff. "I am a Methodist." Sunday attendance at Saint James Methodist Church in Ocean Springs was mandatory for my father growing up, but when I was a kid the only reason he went to church was to drop me off for Sunday school.

It was my best friend, Brenda, who introduced me to God. I was four. She was eight and lived in my maternal grandparents' trailer park with her mom, dad, several rabbits, and a dog that scared me. To say that I worshipped her is to put it mildly. She knew everything.

When Brenda fell in love with Shaun Cassidy, I did too. When she picked out cowl-neck sweaters and velour V-necks from the Sears catalogue, I begged my mom for the same. And in the summer of 1977, Brenda signed up for Bible camp, and I tagged along. Before school started up again, we were both saved. Jesus was our new crush and we competed for his favor. We never swore or took the Lord's name in vain. We went to Sunday school. We always, always, praised God.

Maybe Dad had had enough of Methodism or maybe he didn't feel embraced in our South Jersey congregation because there were so few other Black congregants. But whatever had kept him at bay disappeared when we moved. In richer, Whiter, more conservative Morristown, my parents joined the African Methodist Episcopal church, Bethel AME.

Our new minister had striped gray-and-white hair that accumulated in a widow's peak and a way of pounding on the pulpit, pointing at the sky, and rolling a simple three-letter word like "God" from the pit of his stomach out through his mouth like gathering thunder. Services ran at least two hours and we rarely missed a week. Before I graduated college, Dad took a second retirement and began studying to become an AME minister. By 2001, he was Reverend Ford, just like his grandfather.

Some things our minister said made me pensive and weepy. Still, I loved Genesis and Revelations, and church was a haven for me, a place where my Blackness and my position in my family weren't questioned. For those two-plus hours a week, I fit in almost completely. At nineteen, desperate to be tethered to something, I was baptized in the faith chosen by my father and begun by a former slave.

Soon after my baptism, I visited Brenda. She had moved to southern Florida, so I timed the trip with my college's spring break. I stumbled off the train at the West Palm Beach station full of booze. There was Brenda, her same wide smile and dimpled cheeks. "Praise Jesus," she said.

We went to Bible study, to the fancy Palm Beach mall, and to Key West, where the poor condition of our room and the openly gay men challenged Brenda's normally sunny demeanor. Then, on my last day, we went to church again. It was Palm Sunday and despite all the pastel hats I was in a somber state. I hadn't had a drink in a week and Brenda's constant barrage of evangelism was taking its toll. For several days, I'd heard how that time we got saved didn't count because we didn't do it the right way. According to Brenda, we had to speak in tongues. When I started crying in church, she began to fervently praise Jesus. She mistook those tears as signs of my inner transformation, but they were something else. As parishioners collapsed on the floor full of the Holy Spirit, I cried because I felt hollow.

That night, I left Florida, and a storm blew in as soon as our plane was in the sky. The man in the seat next to me told me that this was his first airplane ride and wondered, "Is it always like this?" I told him it wasn't. He crossed himself, and for the second time that day I cried. I was sure I was about to die. I was afraid to drown because death wouldn't be instant. I'd have to struggle for who knew how long before I could finally succumb. But mostly I was afraid of God. And I was tired of it.

The shaking and the jostling never let up so I kept my eyes shut for most of the flight. Near its end, a warm hand covered mine. The man beside me asked, "Do you mind?" I said, "No. Thank you."

Less than a year later, I stopped drinking.

I wonder what made my great-great-grand-uncle Charles Stuart pledge to "not drink any spiritous or malt liquors, wine or cider," then sign his name under the six original Washingtonian members? The signers described their society as "for our mutual benefit, and to guard against a pernicious practice which is injurious to our health, standing and families." I wonder what was going on with his family.

AFTER DEVANY WAS BORN, WE JOINED A UNITARIAN UNIVERSALIST congregation founded in 1897 by mothers interested in liberal and tolerant religious instruction for their children.[2]

The UU Association had just elected its first Black president, William Sinkford, who called for a reckoning with the organization's history. "We have many stories to uncover—genocide, slavery, oppression," Sinkford said at their general assembly in 2007. "Only by knowing our truths can we act boldly on our spiritual journey of healing."

In Neighboring Faiths class, my daughters visited temples, Christian churches, and mosques. Starting in kindergarten, a program called Our Whole Lives taught them about sexuality. I wanted my daughters to have a relationship both with a higher power and with their bodies. I wanted this for myself too.

The church put together a lecture series, and Margaret Sanger was one of its earliest speakers. Booker T. Washington, Langston Hughes, W. E. B. Du Bois, and Pauli Murray all spoke here as well. Murray would have stood under the gold-plated chalice above our altar, which catches the light coming through the earth-tone stained-glass windows. It was 1968 when she made her address, before she became an Episcopal priest but after she'd written *Proud Shoes*, the memoir of her enslaved and enslaving family, and a resource book that was key to overturning the separate-but-equal laws. When she couldn't get a job as a lawyer because no one wanted to hire a Black woman, she did some freelancing. The women's division of the Methodist Church hired her to compile a pamphlet on where segregation was legal. She gave them a seven-hundred-plus-page document, *States' Laws on Race and Color*, that Thurgood Marshall called "the Bible" for civil rights lawyers.

The United Methodist Church's archives are at Drew University, about halfway between where I live now and where I was living when I first heard of Josephine. One day when school let out early for winter break, Devany came with me to look through their holdings.

Just as you have to go through enslavers to find out about the people they enslaved, you have to go through the husbands to find the wives. No one knew if James, the man who gave us the Ford name, had siblings, who his parents were, or if they and James had been enslaved. His religious life, I hoped, would shed some light on him and Josephine.

Before he became Josephine's husband, in 1879, James entered the Methodist Episcopal Church "on trial," appointed to Columbia, Mississippi. He would have been just seventeen—my dad's age when he joined the Air Force, how old I turned in Brazil. There was a yellow-fever epidemic that year and the economy was suffering, but churches in the area were doing well. James had to find a job, but he kept failing his entrance exam.

After his first failed attempt to become a full-fledged minister, he was named a Sunday school agent, and his discussions were referred to by one annual conference writer as "the best I ever heard." It was five years before he was fully accepted to the ministry. His appointments took him to every part of vast Mississippi, from Columbia to Biloxi. It made me feel sorry for Josephine, who must have raised their six children basically on her own.

James appeared frequently in the Methodist Church's catalogs and newspapers. "Brother James Ford is standing in the breach of the circuit, guiding with firm purpose and a steady hand," one minister wrote in the *Southwestern Christian Advocate*. Thomas Keyes of Ocean Springs wrote about what a fine sermon James had given for Easter. The presiding elder said that my great-grandfather "has succeeded in building up a parsonage and is much loved by the people." He called James a good man.

By 1920, when James was fifty-eight, he'd switched occupations. The census says he was a general laborer then. By 1923, he was listed in the conference's "roll of honored dead." That year, two of his children received distributions of $10.50 each. Probably Burton and Clarence, since they would have been young enough to still be living at home.

The conference typically published memoirs or biographies of their ministers upon death, but though he served thirty-three years in the ministry and "was much loved by the people," there were none for my great-grandfather.[3]

CHAPTER 12

GOOD AS COUSINS

In the winter of imperfect archives, our daughters sledded down hills and built cardboard forts in our basement, and wore out *The Princess and the Frog* DVD while Monique and I kept searching.

Monique posted on AfriGeneas ("Looking for Tempy Burton") and enlisted a Find a Grave volunteer to locate her great-great-grandfather Alfred Burton Stuart's resting place. I joined a local Daughters of the Confederacy email list. I thought of Essie Mae Washington-Williams, the biracial daughter of staunch segregationist Strom Thurmond, who applied to the United Daughters of the Confederacy in 2004 "not to honor the soldiers that fought for a Southern way of life dependent on slavery, but to explore her genealogy and heritage."[1] I thought of historian Saidiya Hartman "straining against the limits of the archive."[2] I thought of the Black women artists who had reached into the more problematic and sometimes racist narratives gathered by the Federal Writers' Project, reimagined them, and offered up their own stories—like *Daughters of the Dust* and *Beloved.*

The Federal Writers' Project was one of the programs of the Works Progress Administration, which put about eight million Americans to work during the Depression doing everything from building bridges and roads to painting murals and collecting ex-slaves' narratives. One WPA worker in Ocean Springs, Mississippi, interviewed formerly enslaved Nat Plummer.

"See dat house over yonder? Dat's de old W. R. Stewart house. Well, de Yankees went dere and got a man wiz hidin' dere. Dey called him a conscript." Plummer went on to say how his old master was good to him, that when he died, the old master's son took over and was good too. Plummer was ninety-six when he gave the interview. He knew my great-great-grandfather's house, so he must have known Tempy. I wondered if the interviewer was White or with the United Daughters of the Confederacy. Some of their members had joined the Federal Writers' Project to propagate a story about slaves loving their masters. If Zora Neale Hurston or another Black WPA employee had been asking the questions, maybe Plummer would have given more details about his life, trusted more, spoken freely.

As I continued transcribing Big Will's papers, I paid close attention to any mention of the Howcotts, McCauleys, and Handys, the Stuarts' in-laws. Members of an enslaved family were often dispersed among their captors' extended family. These in-laws could lead to the rest of Tempy's relatives. As Hurston put it in *Their Eyes Were Watching God*, "Us colored folk is branches without roots and it makes things come round in queer ways."

This is the queer way we finally found the in-laws: through a photograph on a Howcott genealogy website in England—a picture of a Confederate monument in Canton, Mississippi, erected by William Hill Howcott to a boy his family had enslaved, Willis. William Hill Howcott and Elizabeth McCauley Stuart were cousins. They grew up together in Canton. William Hill would become the executor of Elizabeth's estate and make sure she had a proper tombstone next to her husband's in Evergreen Cemetery. I'd read about so-called Black Confederates, that tens of thousands of Blacks had fought for the Confederacy, but I'd dismissed the narrative as propaganda. In trying to rewrite history, the Daughters had erected monuments to the Confederacy decades after the Civil War. But this Howcott monument was unlike anything I'd ever read about or seen: one that honored an enslaved person who had accompanied Confederate soldiers. William Hill Howcott's inscription read, "A tribute to my faithful servant and friend, Willis Howcott, a colored boy of rare loyalty and faithfulness, whose memory I cherish with deep gratitude."

When I reached out to the owner of the genealogy site, he suggested I get in touch with a man, Joel Brink, in New Mexico who had written a book about the Howcotts of Canton and New Orleans. The book, it turned out, included a copy of the picture of my ancestors that I'd found on the internet.

"I've always wondered whether those two girls were children of Colonel Stuart and Tempy Burton," Joel, an art historian, wrote in his first email to me. Joel's wife, Joan, is William Hill Howcott's great-granddaughter. William Hill and his cousin Elizabeth's grandparents were Hill Jones and Judith Boddie Jones, the first people we know of to have enslaved Tempy. And the monument's honoree, Willis, was passed down to William Hill via his grandfather, just like Tempy was passed down to Elizabeth.

Joel found the Stuart family picture the same way I did, online, and reproduced it in the book about his wife's lineage. He thought I'd like to see pendant oil portraits of the Colonel and Elizabeth, whom he called "Cousin Lizzie." The portraits were painted in 1861 by G. P. A. Healy, a renowned artist of the time. (Healy's painting of Abraham Lincoln is still in the White House archives.) The Colonel's and Lizzie's portraits originally hung in the Stuart sitting room in Ocean Springs, next to portraits of the Colonel's father, brother, and his brother's wife. Elizabeth bequeathed the pendants to William Hill and they remain in the Howcott family. Joel didn't know what had become of the others.

Passed down. Bequeathed. I had not seen the portraits. I also had not truly considered our connection when I'd contacted Joel. I ordered two copies of his book, thanked him for sharing what he knew, and wished Joan my best, "as we are as good as cousins"—not exactly blood family, but linked through history.

After the pictures, Joel sent me both a will in which Tempy was bequeathed as property to an heir and an appraisal of her cash value—a bone-chilling document that listed "Tempy a woman & child, year old" for $1,600. The child was Josephine's big brother and Monique's ancestor, Alfred. Monique and I helped our new cousin, too, sending Joel obituaries of Elizabeth's relatives that we'd found in the Stuart Papers. Together we were reclaiming our kin.

Then Joel found the thing I most wanted: a funeral notice for Josephine. I'd pieced portions of her life together through a paper trail and two family heirlooms—married in 1894, traveled to Bath City in Michigan with Tempy in 1905, still alive in Ocean Springs in 1920 with her husband James and four of their six children. But after that she disappeared. Information in the funeral notice enabled me to obtain Josephine's death certificate, which told me how she'd died (from tuberculosis) and in what year (1922). She was only forty-seven, an age I was fast approaching.

The death certificate also contained a very rare thing for African Americans with slavery in their family history: documentation of Josephine's White parentage. The certificate listed the Colonel as Josephine's father. "The archive of slavery rests upon a founding violence," Hartman writes. I had the kind of documentation that mattered to White people. I felt so validated, and also ashamed that I had ever questioned my grandfather's story. The oral history that Black people rely on because often it's all that remains should have been enough for me. The absence is the story.

It was the local Ocean Springs historian who had found Josephine's funeral notice, the will, and the deed, at Joel's request. Odd, since I'd contacted the historian several times myself without luck.

We had luck now, though. On Good Friday, I found Renee Smith on LinkedIn. Then, a Find a Grave volunteer found Tempy in Evergreen Cemetery in "a shaded area where the sun came through just on her headstone." When Joel said he was coming to visit his brother, who lived only twenty minutes from Monique, I knew we had to meet.

It was a misty spring afternoon. When Monique and I arrived, Joel was standing at the top of his brother's long driveway, his white hair pulled back in a ponytail and his arms spread wide to greet us. No sooner had we hugged like family reunited than he got down to business: Had we heard the rumor that one of Tempy's sons had been lynched?

"I didn't know if I should tell you before lunch," he said as we drove toward a restaurant in town. Everything was so damp and green. In the back seat, I felt like a caught fish, as if someone had sunk a hook into my chest and was pulling.

At the quaint country inn, I could not stop thinking about Tempy's son. Had he been dark-haired and handsome? Or had he been fair skinned, and would this have been a help or a hindrance? Did the lynching have to do with a White woman? I stared at my plate and the Shaker chairs around the dining room and tried to guess at how the other people there were connected to each other. Tempy had probably never sat down at a table and been served food the way I was being served. I'd read about how some people had gone to lynchings as if they were circus acts, gathering their children, packing a picnic lunch, taking pictures. Now Tempy's decision to stay with the Colonel and Lizzie after her emancipation was even more unsettling. I could barely speak. But Joel kept the conversation going. He told us how he'd met his wife while they were both in college, how they had lived in Italy while he earned his master's degree, how his children were artists like their mom.

Then he began to talk about his wife's great-grandfather, William Hill. He had acquired land from his cousin Elizabeth in 1913, including lots known as the Stuart Tract, and was named executor of her estate when she died in 1925. The Gulf property was still in Joel's wife's family. The land was sitting on one of the biggest natural oil and gas reserves in the Gulf region, Joel told us while we waited for dessert. Oil was still seeping into the Gulf of Mexico from the Deepwater Horizon spill the previous week, the largest oil spill in the country's history. I don't remember the rest of the lunch. Hook. Fish. Pull.

Before leaving, Joel gave me a gift: an antique silver child's cup that had belonged to Elizabeth's sister. "We want to pass this on to you as a family memento. It is to remind us of the connection that once existed and that has been renewed," his wife had written to me on a handmade card. This was my first correspondence from her.

The cup fit perfectly in my palm; I balanced it there, trying to imagine Tempy holding it. I could see her face in its shiny surface, stoic and calm. In relief on the front of the cup was a child's face surrounded by flowers. It was so similar to one given to us when Dezi was born. Kissing the cup on the side where there was no decoration, I silently thanked Tempy for being so strong, for bringing children into a world that refused to promise them even their basic humanity. The gift was well intended, but it felt to me like a burden. I did not want to have to thank Joel and his wife for something my great-great-grandmother may have polished while living in unpaid bondage to their family. I didn't want to comb through any more of their family's wills and deeds, documents in which Tempy was passed down through the generations along with cattle and farm equipment, for the tiniest bit of information about my family.

In pictures of the three of us from that day, we all look happy. Joel is in the middle, Monique and me on either side of him. Looking at that photo now, there is no way to tell that I had been thinking that day about my hair and how my braids would be received in rural Pennsylvania, or oil invading the beaches of Ocean Springs, or never speaking to Joel again.

The day we met with Joel, the *New York Times* published an op-ed by Henry Louis Gates Jr. claiming that "the problem with reparations may not be so much whether they are a good idea or deciding who would get them; the larger question just might be from whom they would be extracted." But I know that the issue is not about who is to blame. The United States has already shown that it knows who is to blame.

In 1783, the Massachusetts General Assembly approved Belinda Royall's request for a pension from the proceeds of her former enslaver's estate. Almost a century later, Henrietta Wood sued the man who had kidnapped her into slavery and won $2,500—about $65,000 in today's money. After consulting with a group of Black clergy, General William Tecumseh Sherman created Special Field Order 15, which gave newly emancipated slaves forty acres of land and a rented mule as a form of reparations and aid. But just months after its implementation, Lincoln was assassinated and new president Andrew Johnson halted the plan. The land given to Black families along the South Carolina, Georgia, and Florida coast was returned to Confederate landowners.

Who is to blame is not the problem surrounding reparations for slavery. The real question is not from whom reparations should be extracted but what we, the descendants of the enslaved, want—what would help make us feel whole.

Joel's wife's family wanted to restore William Hill Howcott's monument to Willis. In the century since it was erected, it had fallen on hard times. The family hoped to clean off the graffiti and move it to a safer place. It seemed appropriate, Joel wrote me in an email following our meeting, that his two new African American friends would be involved in this restoration. He wanted to know what we thought of the copy to be etched onto the newly restored monument: "Restored by the Descendants of William Hill Howcott, a modest family man of great generosity who embodied in his actions the spirit of brotherly love and racial harmony."

Real racial harmony would have been to release Willis from slavery as soon as he was "inherited," then fight with the Union to end the institution instead of with the Confederates to uphold it. How could I tell this to Joel? How could I not tell this to Joel? Why did I have to be in contact with Joel in the first place? While my petitions to the Ocean Springs historian for help finding Josephine had mostly been met with silence, Joel's had been answered. They were both White, male historians, old enough to be my father, with access to something I desperately wanted: information. If either of them was to come across a family bible detailing Tempy's family's arrival to the United States from Africa, they were under no obligation to reveal that or turn it over to me. For all I knew, maybe Joel's wife and in-laws weren't so happy about our research.

I vacillated between two plans: hiring a lawyer to track down the Gulf property and see if we were owed any money, or going back into therapy and trying to forget. I ran for miles around our county park, wrote angry emails that I would never send and letters in longhand that I burned, but I was still furious.

I exchanged rage with Monique in the rice and cereal aisle at the grocery store. "What would make him tell us about that property?" I asked her. "Couldn't he see how pissed off that would make us? Couldn't he have found a better way to tell us about the lynching? I mean, right before lunch? Who does that?"

Nobody does that. Nobody I'd ever known talked about lynchings. Especially not Black and White people connected through slavery.

The AA *Big Book* says anger is the dubious luxury of normal men and can lead an alcoholic back to drinking. The alcoholic can't afford it. I could not afford it. It wasted my time, confused me, blew me off course. I say anger is the luxury of White men and I resent it, am repelled by it.

The Ocean Springs historian was angry with me because I did not tell him about the Healy portraits. When I emailed to thank him for giving Joel the documents about my family, he responded with an email entitled "hurt feelings." If I wanted help finding Josephine, I'd just have to be patient, he said, or else I'd have to find myself another gofer. Why would I have contacted him about discovering these portraits when he'd only responded to one of my emails over the course of two years? How was I treating him like a gofer when he'd never fetched anything for me? What did he mean by being patient?

Boiling with questions, I paid a visit to my minister. The only other time I'd dropped in on his office unannounced was when I was struggling in my marriage. He understood why I was angry. He reached into the shelves lining the wall behind his desk and gave me a book written by a woman from our town who'd since passed away and was also descended from a Confederate and an enslaved woman. I took the book into my hands like he'd passed me an elixir that would expel the curse that had come down on my house. I read the book in two days. It was a stunning tribute to the woman's mother, who had worked tirelessly for the civil rights of Black people in our now well-integrated town, but it held no secrets for coming to terms with very alive people.

I knew Joel meant well. His book didn't shy away from some dark spots in the family's history, like a connection to Joan's distant relative, the villain of Harriet Jacobs's slave narrative, *Incidents in the Life of a Slave Girl.* But it did not address how the involuntary labor of enslaved people like Willis and Tempy had helped his family to rise.

I had never invited Joel on this journey with me. I had never asked him to contact the local historian. I had not invited him to speak about the Howcott family's land wealth with me, the descendant of people counted among that family's property, or to bring up the violent death of Tempy's son so abruptly, without warning. All I had asked him for were two copies of his book, which I had paid for. Why was I the one who felt like I owed him something when his wife's family had enslaved mine?

Finally I sent Joel a simple, polite email saying that I was sure Joan's great-grandfather would be proud of his family's efforts to restore the monument to Willis. I didn't know what he'd meant by us participating in the restoration, so I didn't refer to it. Then I posted online to ask for help in finding my great-great-grandmother's son Warren, who might have been lynched. I listed the online databases of lynching victims in the United States that I had already checked, all digital versions of Ida B. Wells's 1895 *A Red Record.* None in Jackson County, Mississippi, had the surname Stuart or

Stewart, as it was often misspelled, and none had the first name Warren.

Joel responded to my blog post. He was concerned that I was putting "unverified material on the internet," which came down to "the question of academic/historical ethics." I guess, he wrote, that "in this age of the blogosphere, anything goes . . . with or without permission and without solid source work."

Permission. To search for information about my own family. Is that gatekeeping, gaslighting, White privilege and paternalism, or all of the above? These were all forms of trying to control me, and they were working. As Nell Irvin Painter writes, "Submission and obedience, the core values of slavery, are also the key words of patriarchy and piety."[3] I deeply believed that Joel was the key to getting what I needed. I deeply feared that I would not get what I needed if I alienated him. I was brought up to think this way and I bet Joel was too.

I thought then of the Highland Park municipal judge who had called me "unprofessional" when I'd asked him for a comment on a story I was writing. The town's human rights commission was conducting an investigation to see if he should be allowed to continue in his post since he belonged to a country club that was known to discriminate. What did he think? He thought I had a nerve calling his house. "I have no respect for a newspaper that would hire someone like you," he said. After he'd hung up, his wife had called me, shouting. My editor kept coming by my cubicle to ask when my story would be ready; it was slated for the front page, above the fold, and he had held up the presses. I told him I was still writing, but I was not still writing. I was just trying not to cry. I'd thought, as a journalist, that I was doing a public service. What kind of a person was I?

While Joel and I were emailing about the lynching, the Texas school board was pushing to rename the slave trade the "Atlantic Triangular trade" in textbooks. The United Daughters of the Confederacy kept sending me announcements for picnics and grave-marking ceremonies. Sometimes the whole email was just a query in the subject line: "Does anybody have a hand bell?" I was at my limit. I was done straining against these archives.

If someone in my family had died violently, I had a duty to "shine the light of the truth on it."[4] I shouldn't have to run it by anyone, and especially not the descendants of my family's enslavers. I definitely should not have to tiptoe around their feelings. I had already wasted so much time strategizing about how to navigate a fucked-up situation I hadn't caused, convinced that I had to bend to gatekeepers.

I never responded to Joel's email about permission and historical evidence. It was time, I knew, for me to center my grandmothers, the only gatekeepers I would bow to. It was time for them to take back their story.

CHAPTER 13

JUNETEENTH

Mr. Editor: I desire to find my people. Mother's name was Eliza Burton, sisters, Nancy, Polly, and Liberia Burton. I had a brother Albert Burton who died, and two aunts, Peggy Manrow and Bettie Matthews."

This is how Tempy begins her June 4, 1891, ad in the *Southwestern Christian Advocate*. The ad appeared in a column called Lost Friends, which helped the formerly enslaved find their lost family, taken from them by slavery. The New Orleans paper, serving Southern, Black Methodist Episcopalians, asked that "pastors will please read the requests . . . from the pulpits, and report any cases where friends are brought together by means of letters in the Southwestern."[1]

One hundred and twenty years later almost to the date of Tempy's ad, a complete stranger who likes to sit down on Sunday mornings with historic newspapers and her coffee was struck by it. So she checked the AfriGeneas message boards to see if anyone was looking for Tempy now in the way that Tempy had been looking for her people then. She found Monique. When Monique called me with the news—we had promised each other that we'd unwrap big finds together—I was getting ice cream with Dennis and the girls. I sat down in the parking lot, floored by joy and disbelief as we read the emails together into our phones. Because of this extensive trail of longing, Tempy, her mother, aunts, and siblings, Josephine, Monique, and I all were found.

Tempy asked that any response be sent to her care of "W.R. Stewart, Esq." Most ads requested that letters be sent to the searcher's church or minister. Why did she want the Colonel, who was bound up in this fissure in her family, to be involved in the mend? Perhaps the Colonel had been one of those not entirely inhumane slaveholders that Harriet Jacobs likened to angels' visits—few and far between. Jacobs spoke of her first mistress kindly, "almost like a mother"; they sewed together and the woman even taught Jacobs to write.[2] The Stuarts hadn't taught Tempy to read, but it seemed likely that Elizabeth and the Colonel had shown her some form of kindness. Perhaps they'd just refrained from beating her and that had made her trust them enough to continue working for them and involve them in her personal life when she became free.

"It is also reasonable to suppose that there might have been some kind of attachment formed by living together in this way for years," Henry Bibb, a formerly enslaved man, wrote of his wife, Malinda, who chose to stay with her once enslaver when slavery ended instead of reuniting with him. Bibb speculated that the child Malinda and her enslaver had had together was holding them together. "It is quite probable that they have other children according to the law of nature, which would have a tendency to unite them stronger," he wrote.[3] Maybe Tempy couldn't stand the idea of losing any more family.

Stories of reunifications that took place as a result of these advertisements are scarce "and those that document what happened after the initial moments of joy are more rare still," Heather Andrea Williams writes in *Help Me to Find My People: The African American Search for Family Lost in Slavery*. But a few months after publishing her ad, Tempy reported, "The *Southwestern Christian Advocate* has been the means of recovery of my sister, Mrs. Polly Woodfork and eight children."

I thought of Dezi, not even two years old, sitting on our front lawn as we waited for Dennis to return from a month-long business trip. I'd been worried about the trip because Dezi was so young. Would she forget her father? She was newly walking then and liked to take a few sure steps and then sit down, as if to say, *That's enough right now.* She knew her limits. To pass the time, I'd been coaxing her to walk a bit with me, but she wanted to be still, until her dad pulled up in the driveway. When he got out of the car, she stood up, let out a horrified and ecstatic scream, then took the most consecutive steps she had until that point—at least thirty. Her father gathered her into his arms and she wept, red relief on her wet face. How wonderful and horrible it must have been for Tempy to reunite after so many years with her sister. An exhalation of barely-allowed-to-breathe-in-the-air-of-hope dreams.

Tempy was enslaved until she was in her forties and a 1900 census states that she could neither read nor write. So someone else had carefully crafted her petition and sent it in to the *Southwestern*, then thanked the paper and prayed for it to receive a thousand more subscriptions. Now that I knew where to look, I searched through the New England Historic Genealogy Society's digitized collection of the *Southwestern* for anything written by anyone closely connected to Tempy. Several entries came up by Josephine Burton.

"Dear Uncle Cephas, I am a girl sixteen years old. I take the Southwestern and enjoy reading it. My sister died April 18, 1889." Josephine wrote her first letter to the *Southwestern Christian Advocate* in the 1890s, when she was a teenager. At first, her notes were two- or three-line missives to "Uncle Cephas," the editor who oversaw the column Our Children's Legion for Our Boys and Girls. The Methodist Episcopals were big on education, and this column was probably one of the ways they promoted literacy among children who were one generation removed from institutionalized illiteracy. Sharing the paper with their parents, so many of whom were newly free and probably could not read, was a way for the kids both to learn and to help teach.

By the time she was almost nineteen and soon to be married, Josephine was writing editorials. They're very spicy. She writes things like, "A bold and specious humanitarianism is destroying worship" and "Heart sins that are not opposed, not warred against, arrest prayer."

I got lost in the antique type, the formal language, and tried to understand what exactly was destroying worship, envisioned all the things she must have been up against: enslaved and enslaver parents, outlawed genes, a lynched brother, being the youngest. Even using a different name while her brother went by Stuart must have been challenging. Until she married, Josephine was a Burton, like her mother, and a writer.

"I was at the camp meeting Saturday night and heard Rev. I. Pratt preach a most excellent sermon," she wrote in one edition of the paper. "All my family belongs to the ME church except one," she said in another. "Brother, truly God is good to the children of men. Why can't they serve him?"

I feel sorry for whoever "they" were who wouldn't serve him. And who could it have been? Not the Colonel—he attended church regularly. Probably not Alfred, since his wife helped out with church activities and maybe even joined Josephine in the church's Epworth League for young people. Warren, maybe, or Violet? In private, Josephine must have let them have it. Religion was her battle cry and she had no problem calling you out if you weren't praising right. Materialists and the lascivious were objects of scorn in her editorials; so were foxhole congregants. Dropping in on the church every now and then was no way to live. Josephine proposed a "holy every day life." Her first preoccupations were the same as mine had been: praying right, living right, doing what she could to follow Jesus's example. She'd call you out for other things too. Between the newspaper's column condemning separate but supposedly equal rail cars for Blacks and a report that the annual Colored Methodist Episcopal conference had voted against admitting women, there is this notice by Josephine, published on March 17, 1892: "Miss Josephine Burton, of Ocean Springs, Miss., justly complains against certain persons who have been writing letters to this paper in her name."

She was bold, just as I'd imagined the first time Grandma Lillie Mae had told me about her. Just like the main character in *Iola Leroy*—two righteous mixed girls taking no mess. The book came out in 1892, when Josephine was seventeen. I read it when I was eighteen. I bet she read it too.

IN THE SUMMER OF 1887, REVEREND JAMES FORD PLACED AN ad in the paper announcing an upcoming camp meeting in Ocean Springs. He must have anticipated Black MEs coming from all major cities because he gave details about train fares from Mobile and New Orleans, noting that the trains would stop right at the campground. Josephine would have been twelve then. When she was sixteen, she wrote to the paper to gush about how great her camp meeting was. Two years later, the paper reported that James was appointed to the periodical committee. When he and Josephine married in 1894, they invited the *Southwestern* editor to the ceremony. "We acknowledge receipt of invitation and wish the happy pair very much joy," the editor replied via the paper. Their wedding announcement in the next issue was simple and sweet, the way love should be.

When her niece "little Frankie" died two months shy of her second birthday, Josephine placed a one-line announcement in the *Southwestern*. A week later, she likely penned the unsigned poem about her brother Alfred's infant daughter who "faultered by the way-side and the angels took her home."

Josephine's first letter to the *Southwestern* mentions the death of her sister, but not which one. Pauline would have been twenty-one and May sixteen. I wonder if Tempy was nodding at her lost sister Polly when she named her daughter Pauline.

"If I regard iniquity in my heart, the Lord will not hear me," Josephine wrote in an editorial called "Hindrances to Prayer," quoting Psalm 66:18. I recognized the lyric poetry of the Psalms, my entryway to the Bible as a child, obscuring their grave meaning: "Thou has caused men to ride over our heads / we went through fire and through water / through the greatness of thy power shall thine enemies submit themselves unto thee." Now it sounds less like song and more like war to me.

"Divine grace alone can sustain the soul when the burden is heavy, and care and trial meet us at every step," she wrote on June 29, 1893. "When trial, discouragement and disaster all combine to render the life-path dreary then the blessed faith in Christ alone can hold those unpleasant influences in check and still the troubled waters." Josephine composed her letters in the way of a righteous teenager, the one so many of us use before we learn to be afraid. I can picture her coming home from church one day, sitting down with her mother, and saying, "We're going to find your family."

A few months after her mom and aunt were reunited, on January 1, Emancipation Day, Josephine threw a party. I thought it might have been to celebrate their found family, but it's described in the paper as an event to honor Josephine's pastor, Reverend I. C. Rucker. She was assisted by Mrs. A. B. Stuart and Miss Violet Matthews, her sister-in-law and her sister. I wonder which was the bigger holiday at the time for Blacks—Emancipation Day, the celebration of the Emancipation Proclamation that officially took effect on January 1, 1863—or Juneteenth—June 19, 1865, when, two and a half years after slavery officially ended, the last slaves learned they were free.

When she was in kindergarten, Dezi got a chance to play Juneteenth in front of the whole school for an assembly. Her teacher pulled me aside a week beforehand, embarrassed that in her thirty years as an educator who had majored in history she'd never heard of it. She was White and was looking for some salvation in me, but I couldn't give it. I'd only heard about the holiday myself a few years before that, when my in-laws had come for a visit and—as we listened to the news that the US delegation would not apologize for slavery at the upcoming UN World Conference Against Racism—asked me why Black people hadn't gotten over slavery yet.

There is no getting over, there is only getting through. Tempy's petition was heartbreak and nourishment and Josephine's offerings to the *Southwestern* were like love letters, an inheritance that was no tax and all profit, that bound me to her in the right kind of belonging. I printed out the ad, the response, and Josephine's first note to the *Southwestern* and tacked them to the corkboard in my office, where they remain. I turn to them when I get bored or when I need to focus. I bring them with me on trips, and some mornings to my lap when I prepare to meditate.

I like the word Tempy used in her thank-you ad, "recovery," the kind of life I am trying to live.

CHAPTER 14

PLANTATION DIARIES

I f you are going to recover the rest of your enslaved family, you will have to get a PhD in the history of their enslavers. It takes the average student 8.2 years to earn a doctorate degree, so you will need to practice persistence and patience. You will also need to forgive yourself. Daily. Spending this much time with people, even people who are dead, even people who enslaved your ancestors, will inevitably open you to their humanity as you consider their brutality. Forgive yourself for laughing when they poke fun at each other in their letters, for your heart pangs when they lose a child to yellow fever, or your awe at the care their descendants took to preserve their two-hundred-year-old diaries, correspondences, and hand-drawn maps of their land grants. Forgive and proceed.

At the end of the petition to find her people, Tempy wrote, "My mother, sister Nancy, Bro. Albert, aunt Bettie, and aunt Peggy lived on the same plantation and belonged to Dr. Sterling's people. Liberia and Polly belonged to Dr. Robert Hilyard. Liberia was salivated when a child. I left them in Attakapas, La." The Hilliards and Stirlings were movers and shakers. The Hilliards first settled in Kent, Delaware, and by the 1700s they'd established themselves in North Carolina. In 1818, James Hilliard petitioned the state along with thirty-one of his fellow Nash County citizens to amend the slave-patrolling laws because he found the "increasing insolence of the slaves; the growing numbers and influence of free negroes and molatoes: quite alarming." His group also hoped "a law may pass forbidding female free negroes or molatoes from intermarrying with Slaves . . . to keep their progeny free of the parish."[1]

James's interest in slave progeny may have directly affected my family. His wife was Mourning Boddie, first cousin to Judith Boddie, the woman who married Hill Jones and enslaved Tempy. "Tempy," and its variations, was a popular name in the Hilliard and Boddie households. Mourning had a cousin named Tempe and a sister named Temperance, and she and James named their daughter Tempe Boddie Hilliard. James's two sisters, who died young and never married, were named Nancy and Polly, like Tempy's siblings. Slaveholders were known to name slaves after their own family members.

James's niece married someone with the last name of Burton. His nephew, Robert Carter Hilliard, born in 1808, studied medicine in Baltimore, and married Mary Walker in 1837. "Financial reverses" brought Hilliard to sell his dad's once-prosperous plantation and head west. In 1848, he moved the family to the Attakapas region of Louisiana. By 1860, he had a medical practice up and running there and held six slaves.

What's left of Hilliard is the family plantation in Nash, North Carolina, lined with small, black-barked oaks, now listed in the National Register of Historic Places as the Robert C. Hilliard House.[2] There are also a few collections of papers, archived at Louisiana State University and the University of Texas. One of these papers is a slave inventory. "Polly, age 20, value $1000" is listed on line number thirty-three.

The inventory says the slaves belonged to W. E. Walker of Evergreen Plantation in Saint Mary, part of the Attakapas region where Tempy left her family. Walker was probably Hilliard's brother-in-law. It seems that Walker bailed out some of his relatives, buying up their property or paying off their debts in hard times. Maybe he bought up some of Hilliard's slaves when the doctor could no longer afford them. Maybe this Polly is Tempy's sister.

And there's another thing that Hilliard left behind. According to the papers, his wife Mary "renunciated and relinquished any rights she had in her husband's slave, Tempe," because Hilliard wanted to sell her "to some person in the city of New Orleans." That person, Joseph Saul,

bought Tempe for $800 in April 1855. She was sixteen.
This Tempe would be around twenty years younger than
mine. How many Tempes/Temps/Tempys did Hilliard
enslave? Tempy. Temporary. Endlessly disrupted. There is
no way to know the identity of this other Tempe. There
is no way to know if the Polly in the Walker inventory is
my Polly, Tempy's Polly, since she was stripped of her family identity, her last name. If you are going to find your
enslaved ancestors, you may have to reconsider the word
"find" and learn to live with something adjacent. You will
also have to reconsider the word "people."

*Tempy's mother, sister Nancy, brother Albert, aunt Bettie and
aunt Peggy lived on the same plantation and belonged to Dr.
Sterling's people.*

"Dr. Sterling" was Ruffin Gray Stirling, a medical student in New Orleans, licensed in 1858, the same year that
Elizabeth McCauley married Colonel Stuart and just after
Polly appeared in W. E. Walker's inventory. His people
were many: Alstons, Palfreys, Conrads, Hardings, Lobdells,
Rouths, Matthews, Turnbulls. And that's only blood kin and
in-laws, not mentors and close friends, chosen family.[3]

Ruffin's grandfather had passed down an estate the size
of a principality that included slaves purchased in Saint
Mary's Parish. Some of the enslaved shared names with
Tempy's family as listed in her ad. There was Peggy, Nanc,
Nancy, and Temp. "The negroes are to remain together un-
divided until my youngest child shall be twenty-one years of
age," Ruffin's grandfather, Alexander Stirling, wrote in his
1808 will. Ruffin's grandmother echoed the sentiment in

her will in 1832, stating that "my slaves be divided in that manner as near as can be without dividing families which in no case is to be done if it can be avoided." Ruffin's father, Lewis Stirling, inherited both land and slaves, and owned four plantations, one in Attakapas, where sugar was made, where Tempy left her family. He also owned beachfront property in Pascagoula, Mississippi, not far from Ocean Springs, where Colonel Stuart and Elizabeth would settle and three generations of my paternal family were born.

The Stirlings and their people left behind enough documentation to fill a small library. Personal letters, slave birth registries, and plantation diaries charting everything from the weather to how much cotton was picked by each slave was assembled into the Lewis Stirling and Family Papers archived at Louisiana State University. If any information existed about Tempy's mother, Eliza, and the rest of her family, it should be in this collection. A microfilmed copy was available at the Firestone Library at Princeton University, just an hour's drive from me, and ten minutes from my sister.

It was the end of July and hardly anyone was around. Downstairs, I practically had the entire special collections room to myself. I scanned through rows and rows of microfilm. Two centuries of Stirlings, their losses and victories, their painstaking catalog of buying, selling, and mortgaging human beings.

"To guard against the possibility of abuses," Stirling forbade his overseer from "strik[ing] a Negro with the butt end of his whip stick or any other weapon by which the negro might be injured," or punishing "a negro with more than a dozen stripes over his shoulders with the lash of his whip except in extreme cases when he thinks the fault merits a whipping on the naked skin."

It's unclear how Tempy ended up with Hill Jones's granddaughter Elizabeth and the Colonel while the rest of her family stayed with the Hilliards and Stirlings. Especially since Martia Goodson's study of ex-slave interviews found that, of all the relationships slave owners disrupted either through sale or dispersal, they were least likely to separate mothers and daughters. It might have had to do with the fact that Hill Jones's daughter bought a beach home in Ocean Springs not far from the Stirlings, where the sons got "as brown as Indians" and the daughters recovered from headaches and pleurisy.

Only two things I can think of would make someone defy their family: love and money.

"I have sold to Mrs. E. B. Lyons Old Billy, Sylvia, Solomon, Harry, Martin, Billy Boy, Sylvia's Nan, and her child Anderson, Magdalin, and Celeste," Stirling wrote to his namesake, Lewis Stirling Jr., in 1843. "The Negroes will probably be somewhat distressed at being sold and you must say what you can to reconcile them. Tell them (which is the fact) that I owed Mrs. Lyons and had no other way of paying and that I have no doubt they will be as well off with her as with me."

He signed his letter, "Your affectionate Father."

Less than a month later, Stirling used one hundred people he enslaved as collateral to secure a $36,790.94 loan.

They were listed by name, age, descriptions of their color, and often grouped in families. There was a girl named Polly, child of Rachael, who was seven years old, and a girl named Eliza, child of Lucky, age three years, both children "of a black color."

Three hundred and thirty-seven children were born to seventy-nine enslaved women on the Stirlings' Wakefield Plantation before slavery ended. Among the names of the slaves recorded by the Stirlings and related families, I found a handful of Elizas. Eliza on a plantation in Attakapas who had a baby boy who died. Eliza who was born in 1837, dead at twenty. Young Eliza listed in the mortgage. None of them was my Eliza, Tempy's mother. But with every record of them living—the shoes Eliza received in the fall of 1847, the smallpox vaccination she took in 1842—I kept hoping. Somebody's Eliza was there on the page. Somebody's people were listed in this mortgage. One hundred souls. One hundred names.

"It is likely that most people and/or families who lived in Louisiana through the year 1820 regardless of racial designation or status can be found in these databases by name," Dr. Gwendolyn Midlo Hall explains in the introduction to the free online Louisiana Slave Database. The database contains information on over one hundred thousand enslaved people in Louisiana from 1719 through 1820, including where they were born, their African nation and language, if they were involved in running away or revolts against slavery, their skills, and family relationships. But my Eliza wasn't there either.

Still, sorting through those other names, the ones that did line the page—Marie Louise Mulatresse, who was involved in a conspiracy or slave revolt in 1811, or Marenday, wife of Allen, age twenty-five—I became attached to them. I wanted to know if their people had found them the way that woman who read historical newspapers as she drank her coffee wanted to know if Tempy's people had found her. I went through three archives in three states over seven years for seven names.

They weren't my Eliza. They were all my Eliza. Beyond family, deified ancestors, building up to something holy.

ELIZA, OF HEBREW ORIGIN, MEANS PLEDGED TO GOD.

Solomon Northup wrote heartbreakingly of an Eliza in his memoir *Twelve Years a Slave*. (He also makes a passing reference of meeting the slaves from Stuart's plantation. When I came across it, I thought I'd die. But Stuart is never mentioned again.)[4]

Northup's Eliza was enslaved and concubined to Elisha Berry, impregnated by him, promised freedom when he died, then recaptured on the way to get her free papers.

When she was bought by William Ford in New Orleans, she became known as Dradey. Northup was renamed Platt. Ford, "a man above the ordinary height," "cheerful and attractive in his face, and in his tone of voice," a Christian and later a Baptist minister, paid $700 for her and $1,000 for Northup. When it came time for Eliza to leave the slave pen for his place in the Great Pine Woods in "the heart of Louisiana," Ford gazed at her "with an expression indicative of regret at having bought her at the expense of so much sorrow." Days before, Eliza's son Randall had been sold to a planter in Baton Rouge. "The little fellow was made to jump, and run across the floor, and perform many other feats, exhibiting his activity and condition," all while Eliza wailed and wrung her hands, "begging and beseeching them, most piteously not to separate the three. Over and over again she told them how she loved her boy—how very faithful and obedient she would be; how hard she would labor day and night, to the last moment of her life, if he would only buy them all together." But the man could not afford it. Meanwhile, the slave trader called her "a blubbering, bawling wench" and threatened her with a hundred lashes if she didn't stop—he would give her something to cry about.

"Don't cry, mama. I will be a good boy. Don't cry," is the last thing Eliza heard Randall say.

The next day, Eliza, her little girl, Emily, and most every enslaved person in the pen came down with smallpox. Northup almost died.

He wrote: "I have seen mothers kissing for the last time the faces of their dead offspring; I have seen them looking down into the grave, as the earth fell with a dull sound upon their coffins, hiding them from their eyes forever; but never have I seen such an exhibition of intense, unmeasured, and unbounded grief, as when Eliza was parted from her child.

Eliza broke from the line of women, went to Emily, and gathered the girl in her arms until the slave trader struck her so hard she almost fell over." To try to calm Eliza, Ford tried to buy Emily too, but the slave trader said she wasn't for sale. "There were heaps and piles of money to be made of her" when she was a few years older, he said. Men in New Orleans "would give five thousand dollars for such an extra, handsome, fancy piece as Emily would be."

Emily would end up sexually enslaved, as Eliza was.

HERBERT G. GUTMAN STUDIED THE LEWIS STIRLING AND FAMILY collection for his now classic book, *The Black Family in Slavery and Freedom*. The book was a response to Daniel Moynihan's 1965 study, "The Negro Family: The Case for National Action," which claimed slavery had resulted in a "tangle of pathology" among modern Blacks, including a weak family system. Long on rhetoric but short on any real science, Moynihan's report shifted the focus from long-standing institutionalized racism onto Blacks themselves. Psychologist William Ryan later wrote that Moynihan's report blamed the victims. His critique is where the phrase "blaming the victim" comes from.

Gutman's study showed the opposite of a weak family system. "Enslavement was harsh and constricted the enslaved," Gutman writes, "but it did not destroy their capacity to adapt and sustain the vital familial and kin associations and beliefs that served as the underpinning of a developing Afro-American culture."

I read somewhere that people had even reentered slavery just to stay with their families. Black women in particular became enslavers in order to buy their loved ones.

"For . . . the sum of six hundred dollars cash," Stirling's son Lewis Stirling Jr. bought three people from Caroline Perry, a free woman of color. "Negro woman named Ellen aged about 24 years, of a black complexion, girl Esther aged 7 years of griff complexion and boy Alfred aged 4 years of a black complexion to have and to hold." On first read, I thought Perry was buying the family. Once I understood that she was selling them, I wondered if Lewis Jr. had purchased a woman (Ellen) that he'd had children with in order to keep them all nearby.

Lewis Jr., like the Colonel, had several children with women he enslaved. One of those children was Primus. This Black branch of the family dropped the *i* and added an *e* to their last name to become the Sterlings. I kept seeing Primus's name in the mortgages, in the slave birth register. Today, I keep seeing his descendant's name in the news headlines. Primus's great-great-great-grandson, Alton Sterling, was killed in July 2016 by a police officer while he was selling DVDs outside of a convenience store in Baton Rouge.[5]

When you are trying to find your enslaved ancestors, you will lean on the descendants of other people enslaved by the same families. They are another kind of kin. These relatives, the descendants of Primus, delivered the sad news to me about Alton's death just after Independence Day in a family email chain, the way kinfolk do. Alton is a variation of the name Alston, which in Old English means "Old Town." Alton did not stray very far from his old town, his people's old town, the plantation where his people were enslaved by his people. After two centuries, our country had not moved from its old-town ways.

CHAPTER 15
TEMPY'S LOT

The main road advanced and inclined, the Gulf of Mexico opening up as we crested the hill. If it hadn't been for the headlines, and the disaster workers in their neon-orange uniforms, you would never have suspected the spill. There was no smell of oil or any tar balls on the beach. The town was quietly beautiful. Riding there, I hoped that Ocean Springs, the quaint Gulf town where my dad, grandfather, and great-grandmother were born and raised, where the French established their first American outpost, would live up to its nickname: the City of Discovery.

Monique and I slipped out of our sandals, faced the water, and sunk our feet into the sand where Tempy had once walked. I felt unshakable and connected, like a power cord plugged into a socket. I gathered up a good amount of sand in a plastic baggie that Monique had brought along for the occasion.

The beach had been a favorite spot of Lizzie's, and Tempy would have accompanied her here. I hoped Tempy had liked the beach as much as I did and that it wasn't yet another place she had to go because of someone else's need. Then I remembered the beaches had been segregated. She would never have been allowed on the sand without Elizabeth.

Not far from the beach, we stumbled across Stuart Avenue, then Alfred's old property, and, diagonal to it, his daughter Tempy Elizabeth's. Josephine would have spent so much time in these sandy yards where homes doubled as classrooms for Black children before the town built colored schools.[1] A few blocks away was Porter Avenue, where my dad once lived, where the Colonel and Elizabeth used to live and worship at Saint Paul's Church on Sundays. When we told the church secretary about our connection to the place, she ushered us into the sanctuary like we were visiting dignitaries. She took our pictures in front of the stained-glass windows, where newly married couples posed for wedding photos, the Colonel's and Elizabeth's names etched in the bottom.

One of the staff members called Eleanor Lemon, a ninety-four-year-old lifelong member of Saint Paul's. She remembered Lizzie Stuart sitting on a couch in the back of the sanctuary. She also remembered Tempy's granddaughter, Monique's great-grandmother, Tempy Elizabeth. "She used to play the piano," Eleanor said. "Mama would have her come over to the house to play for us sometimes." But she didn't remember Lizzie's constant companion and helper, and she'd never seen the picture of Tempy with the Stuarts and the young girls.

Another staff member called the church's lay historians, a married couple. The wife had seen the Colonel's bible in the church's history closet once and so a search took place, the staff members splitting up to check every storage shelf and cupboard. One called down to Saint Paul's newer, bigger offshoot, but they hadn't seen the book either. After a half hour, the wife conceded that the bible had disappeared. Family bibles were the next best thing to a diary. They often included family trees, and even the names of enslaved people. It took us all several minutes to recuperate from the defeat. Monique and I sat in the neat sitting room adjacent to the sanctuary in stunned silence until the husband offered to drive us to where our people were buried.

The Colonel and Lizzie have plots halfway into Evergreen Cemetery, surrounded by an iron fence, under a canopy of Spanish moss, the bayou to their smooth stone backs. Monique rustled up a crisp handkerchief from her purse while I watched a man in an orange jumpsuit mow the grass to give her some privacy. She silently pressed the handkerchief to her mouth and placed it on the Colonel's tombstone. I only had a couple of business cards, stickers for my girls, and loose change with me. What to leave? I rifled through my change purse and found the heavy anniversary coin I kept from AA. I kissed it on its roman numerals,

XIX, and placed it on top of Monique's delicate hanky so that the delta wind wouldn't blow it away. I almost said, "I forgive you," but that wasn't true. I didn't know what exactly I would be forgiving. I ran my hand across the curb of the headstone, listened to the *ohm* of the lawnmower, then asked God to rest his soul.

Finding Tempy and her children wasn't as easy. Monique continued along the road that cut through the cemetery and I followed the one that hugged the outer perimeter near the marsh, sweat streaming. The footpath had to be below sea level by several feet. I was lower than the graves, walking beneath the remains of my ancestors and so many others, hundreds of years removed from their time on earth and their physical bodies. The mowing stopped, the mosquitoes attacked, and two butterflies flitted back and forth between the lower path and the hill above like they were playing a game.

Mosquito bites bloomed into bright welts on my bare arms and legs. I screamed up to Monique something about yellow fever, Zika, mosquito disease. Monique screamed back: "I found Tempy."

Tempy's headstone was diagonal from the Colonel and Lizzie, overlooking the marsh. The way they were buried, it was like the Colonel and Lizzie were watching over Tempy and her kids. The three-foot tombstone was so white, the marble glistened in the rays of sunlight that managed to peek through the thick shade.

"It's like someone cleaned her up for us," Monique said. "Like she knew we were coming."

I checked and double-checked the name—"Tempe" with an *e* and not a *y*, like on her glass and in her ad—and inspected the stone that had been broken in two places then reset with an ugly-colored clay. I cringed at the words: "Loyal servant faithful to the end." It was so similar to the phrasing on Willis's monument.

Until the 1950s, most public cemeteries in the United States were racially segregated in some way, but this one in Ocean Springs was unique. Evergreen was a public cemetery where Blacks and Whites, Protestants and Catholics were buried. Some people, like the Stuarts, were laid to rest in neat rows in gated plots, others randomly under trees, on a hillock, near the marsh, wherever there was room. I knelt at Tempy's grave and gently grazed it while Monique pulled out rocks we'd painted back home with our girls. We took our turns placing them, taking a few minutes to reflect in silence. Alfred's square stone marker was just to Tempy's left at the base of a tree, also freshly cleaned. To her right was an unmarked slab where an unknown person was buried, the butterflies circling it. I thought of Alice Walker standing in the overgrown field where Zora Neale Hurston was buried and boldly staking a claim to an unmarked grave there for Zora, who had died in poverty, slipped almost into obscurity, and who might have stayed there had it not been for Alice writing about the pilgrimage. Since I knew Josephine was buried somewhere in Evergreen and her family was so near, I claimed the concrete slab as her final resting place and marked it with one of the hand-painted rocks so she wouldn't be alone. I hoped that someone had buried Tempy, Josephine, and the rest of the family pointing home toward Africa, feet facing east.

THE JACKSON COUNTY ARCHIVES IN PASCAGOULA, MISSISSIPPI, located in a one-story brick building, is a repository for the entire county. There had to be documents there as old as our country, so I was surprised when two staffers came out and told us to help ourselves. "You can just spread your stuff out on the table," the younger one said, pointing to a small card table we'd passed when we first came in.

Twenty minutes later, the card table was full and we'd spread out even further, to the tops of metal shelves and cardboard boxes holding documents salvaged from Katrina. There were so many wills, deeds, and court documents on our family that we'd need to live in the cramped office for the rest of the summer to get through them all. I was folded over the table, reading Elizabeth McCauley Stuart's typed-out will, the first bequest of which leaves "my faithful old cook, Tempe Burton, the sum of Five Hundred dollars ($500), with the advice that she use and invest the said money for her best interest and comfort under the advice and direction of W. H. Howcott. In case the said Tempe Burton dies while I am yet living, the said Five hundred dollars ($500) is to be given to her son Alfred, and her daughter Violet, to be equally divided between them."

In the musty archives, still airing out from the flood, the breath of hundreds of years mingling, the will looked different to me. From my computer, it had seemed brutal, mean. Elizabeth was infantilizing Tempy. "Faithful old cook" seemed like a better description for a beloved family pet. But now, I sensed something like affection in the old, typed words. Elizabeth was two years from death when she drew up the will and at the front of her mind was Tempy. Then she thought about Tempy's kids. With their history before me, I realized for the first time that Alfred, Tempy's oldest child, had named his firstborn after both these women: Tempy Elizabeth Stuart. I wondered if Tempy and Elizabeth had been engaged in some kind of partnership. If Elizabeth had been a kind of second mother to Alfred.

Tempy and Elizabeth died just months apart, the way some married couples do. The bulk of their eighty years together spanned Tempy's freedom, not her enslavement. I had only ever thought about Tempy's relationship to the Colonel and what might have made her want to stay with him after slavery had ended. I hadn't considered that she might have wanted to remain with Elizabeth.

The oversize land-record books were in the back of the building next to a table long enough to hold the two-foot ledgers. Monique continued with the registers up front while I looked for James Ford in the cumbersome ones in the back, cradling each tome like a baby. Instead, I found Josephine Ford's name, and Monique found something that neither of us had bargained for: Tempy Burton in the land rolls.

In 1887, Tempy bought a 14,400-square-foot lot of land for $60.[2] Two years later, when Tempy was seventy-eight years old, she paid a dollar to the town to have their records corrected. In fact, she'd paid $60 for an acre of land, about three times the size they'd recorded. I wonder how the error came to her attention since by all accounts she couldn't read. How much did it sting to have to pay a dollar, about $27 today, for the town's mistake?

Then, in 1891, two days after her Lost Friends ad was published, Tempy took out a mortgage with the Southwestern Building and Loan Association for $500 for a lot adjacent to the property she already owned. Colonel Stuart was listed as the trustee and her son Alfred served as a witness. She must have saved her wages after emancipation when she became the Stuarts' cook and Elizabeth's nurse. Maybe she even saved during slavery. Some enslaved people earned money through their skills as seamstresses, carpenters, herbalists, and cooks.

Tempy had paid off that $500 debt in full by 1899 and was continuously listed in the enormous land rolls as a taxpayer on the lot, as late as 1921. Tempy Burton, my once enslaved great-great-grandmother, had been a landowner.

The property meant to be held in trust was later given to Tempy's daughters, Josephine and Violet, in a quitclaim deed for a dollar each. In African cosmology, land is matrilineal and communal. I ran my hand across Tempy's name on the onion-skin paper. How it must have felt for her to go from being owned to owning something.

My Granddaddy Alonzo always said, "You've got to own something." He hoped that someday his five grandkids would come and live on his family land in Arkansas, like we were the Black Ewings from *Dallas*. "I can get the babies ponies," he said to try and bribe us when Dennis and I visited him there, our girls still little. It was tempting. Growing up, Granddaddy Alonzo always doted on me, stopped what he was doing when I would ask him for a ride in his pickup, told me how smart I was when I would read the paper to him after dinner. When he retired to the family farm in Arkansas, we grandkids were each given a piece of what he'd relinquished in New Jersey: a house, a trailer park, and two other small rental properties. I'd let my big sister, who made her living managing property, manage mine as well, a tiny house that needed massive repairs. When I got back from Mississippi, I gave her a dollar and she gave me the title for my allotment of our grandparents' land.

The Colonel was at the end of his life when he acted as trustee on Tempy's mortgage. He'd be dead in three years. His will had probably burned up in a big fire the city had suffered in the late 1890s. There was no trace of it.

Three months after she died, half of Tempy's lot belonged to W. S. VanCleave and he was selling it. I'd expected that Tempy's property would automatically go to her children; several of them were still alive then. Tempy must have assumed the same thing, because she left no will and let the land become heirs' property. But heirs' property is vulnerable to loopholes that speculators and developers regularly take advantage of. According to the US Department of Agriculture, heirs' property is the leading cause of Black involuntary land loss in the country.

By 1926, the state of Mississippi would take control of a piece of Josephine's property through a tax sale. Her son Adrian is listed as the grantor in the transaction. He was able to maintain the other three-quarters of the parcel until at least 1931. Holding on to property, I've learned, isn't easy.

The little house that I'd inherited now had a tree growing in the middle of it. The whole structure needed to come down. Then there were the back taxes. After about three years of paying for a house that was unlivable, I called it quits. Another sibling gave me a dollar to take it off my hands.

DENNIS AND I WERE TRYING TO SELL SOME PROPERTY TO GET out of debt when I went to see Pam, a medium, just before I traveled to Ocean Springs. I'd met her at a house party some writer friends had invited me to that had culminated in a séance.

"There is a green aura around you," Pam said as I walked toward her down the hallway. She had an office in the same building as the EMDR practitioner, two basement mystics. "You must be about to make some money." I was worried about our potential buyer falling through, so I welcomed the prophecy if not her cavalier delivery.

I'd been to plenty of clairvoyants the way some people go to church on high holidays, with a foxhole belief motivated by desperation. Clairvoyants were for the future. Mediums were for the past. Trying to contact the dead, which is what I was interested in, seemed different than divining. The repository I needed, I knew, was in the spirit realm. My grandmothers held the family archive, not Joel, not the Census Bureau. So I'd called on Pam, who'd seemed grounding and kind at the party. I longed now for my grandmothers' blessings.

I asked Pam directly: "Can you talk to my great-great-grandmother, Tempy?" She was skeptical. "There is no way to verify that the spirit is who you hope it is because you've never met your great-great-grandmother," she said.

Many enslaved Blacks mixed Christianity and conjuring. Some carried conjure bags containing important personal objects along with a bit of nature, like roots, vines, or graveyard dirt "to facilitate connection with Ancestors," Tiya Miles writes in *All That She Carried*. "Knowledgeable, respected, and also feared, people accepted as conjurers in enslaved Black communities possessed special skills and responsibilities. Their craft involved divining information and influencing social relations through rituals that drew on the spiritual empowerment of . . . objects."

I didn't have any objects with me, but felt I had gathered enough information to know my great-great-grandmother from other spirits if she showed up.

Pam's eyes darted around the room like they were chasing something. She announced a presence. The first spirit to arrive was a guide—a "long-haired, New-Agey kind of woman," Pam said, who looked Native American. She had been gone for a long time. She brought a man with her who worked with his hands, was happy-go-lucky, and kept talking about jewelry, "a necklace with gems in it that had to do with someone named Maggie." From Pam's description and the messages he delivered through her, I recognized the man as my Granddaddy Alonzo and the woman as his wife's grandmother, Maggie Lively.

Several minutes later, the female spirit with the long dark hair came back, this time guiding another, shorter woman with joint problems and "heart issues at the end," Pam said. The cause of death on Tempy's death certificate was "carcinoma of the left breast." Pam said the first spirit was reading and rifling through a newspaper. I figured the guide had to be Josephine.

"What happened to Tempy's son?" I asked Pam next. "I see fleeing, running, and then falling," she said. "One was running like he was being chased down this very steep slope, woods, running, falling, tragic. Other people have guns. It's either a war or a personal attack." She saw marshes. "It was hot as hell in that area," she said. "There was a legal action with a judge, a decree or something." Pam couldn't tell if it was about land or a crime. War, personal attack, land, crime. It sounded a lot like the history of this country.

CHAPTER 16

CROWD OF SORROWS

The body of Warren Matthews, the negro who was
lynched last night for having attempted to criminal-
ly assault Miss Rosina Fountain of Back Bay . . . was
found this morning hanging from the broken limb of
a persimmon tree. . . . The verdict was that death was
due to strangulation and gunshot wounds inflicted at
the hands of unknown parties. The body was taken
in charge by the man's relatives. The consensus of
opinion was that the lynching was justifiable.

—*Times Picayune,* FEBRUARY 4, 1901

NO ONE SHOULD EVER HAVE TO DO THAT, TAKE THEIR FLESH
and blood's bullet-riddled body, strangulated neck, and find
a way to unhinge it from the broken limb of a persimmon

tree. So many indignities in one short lifetime. Warren, Tempy's youngest son, was thirty-eight. The task of liberating his body from the tree would have fallen to his only brother, Alfred, any of Alfred's sons-in-law, and, if he wasn't out of town preaching, his brother-in-law, James.

The lynching was covered in at least a half dozen articles that appeared in newspapers across the country from as far west as Idaho and east to New Jersey.[1]

A mystery solved. Another family member found. A horrid victory. The same geni friend who had found Tempy's ad had dug up the articles, and emailed only one at first, with an advisory. She had very nearly gotten ill reading some of them and could only imagine what lay ahead for us, his family. So she would wait, she said, until she heard from us before sending the others. I brought the first article into the bathroom to get away from my daughters.

When my neighbor was murdered while we were both in the third grade, my mother tried to keep me from listening to the reports on the news, but I still overheard the TV: *killer was a family friend, strangled, raped.* I still imagine her naked body floating in the creek where we used to play—Kathy alone with the minnows, after dark, our playmate finding her. We were eight then. My daughters were ten and seven the day the lynching articles arrived. I turned on the fan so my kids and husband wouldn't hear me while I wept at the likelihood that it was my great-granduncle, Warren Stuart, who had been lynched, and for all of the other Warren Stuarts whose lives had come to an abrupt end, swinging from trees for the crime of being born Black.

I typed the stanzas of Rumi's "The Guest House" into the email response—*Even if they're a crowd of sorrows*—and asked that she forward the rest of the articles. In one, Warren "Stewart" breaks into a girl's house and drags her outside. In another, he accosts her outside and drags her into her home. In some, she's as old as seventeen; in others, as young as eleven. He raped her. He thought about raping her. He touched her skirt in a way that assured he was about to rape her. He was Warren "Stewart," my uncle, in one, and Warren "Matthews" in others, maybe someone related to Tempy's aunt with the same last name. Whoever he was, according to newspapers in Columbus, Trenton, New Orleans, and Richmond, "the black fiend" deserved to die.

The more I read, the more I knew this had to be Tempy's son Warren and not some relative or similarly named person. The two different last names used in the articles only made it more likely. Warren Stuart appears in the educable children indexes up until 1878, like the rest of his school-age siblings. The Stuart last name was often misspelled "Stewart." (There just so happened to be a Black Stewart family in town, headed by a man named Alfred, adding to the Stuart/Stewart confusion.) In adulthood, Warren named himself and started going by Mathews, like his sister Violet, probably borrowing the surname from their aunt. On the quitclaim deed where Violet's mom conveyed her property and on a declaration for invalid pension application that Warren signed as a witness for his friend who'd fought for the Union Army, the siblings both spell their last name with one *t*. In all likelihood, the newspaper accounts of the lynching misspelled the last name as "Matthews," using the typical spelling. I have never come across a record of any other lynching in Ocean Springs, let alone of another Warren. This brutalized man was surely Josephine's brother.

One article called the event a stain on the town's name. Another reported that about three hundred people were in the crowd. The population of Ocean Springs in 1901 was 1,472 people. On a wintry night, 20 percent of the town turned out to see a hanging. The *Pascagoula Democrat-Star* and the *Scranton Chronicle* published articles about the lynching a week after it happened as well as a ledger of those who participated in the Warren Mathews inquest and what each was paid. The constable, W. D. Bullock, was paid $1, as was the sheriff at the time, Casper Vahle, who served as a witness. Sam Starks and six jurors were paid a total of $6. Thomas W. Grayson, justice of the peace, former mayor, Mason, Methodist, buried in Evergreen with Tempy and the rest of her family, got paid $5. That's just about how much I got paid daily for my jury duty service in 2020.

The *Picayune* reported that Warren had never been in trouble with the Whites in Ocean Springs. He was arrested once for not working on the roads, but paid a fine and moved on. Black men were regularly arrested if they couldn't prove they had a job. Then, if they couldn't afford the heavy fines levied for these infractions, they were sent to forced-labor camps.

I want to say that Warren was lucky he was able to pay his fine, and didn't end up in a mine somewhere or picking cotton under the sweltering Mississippi sun to pay off his debt. But he ended up lynched.

Dad had never heard about the lynching of his great-uncle, but he didn't doubt it. "Ocean Springs was the kind of place where all the niggers knew their place," he said.

I couldn't remember my father ever having used that word before, except maybe to quote Richard Pryor. It was a shock and a blessing at once. We were sitting in my parent's kitchen, where Grandpa Martin had slipped that macaroni necklace around my neck and given me the courage to ask him about our past. Only now, the kitchen was bigger and had a deck where tomatoes were growing from some contraption Dad had ordered through cable TV.

"Mississippi always frightened me," Dad said. "I never felt comfortable there. Never." Mississippi had the highest number of lynchings in all the years they'd been recorded by the NAACP. On April 24, 1960, at Biloxi Beach, more than one hundred Black men, women, and children were attacked and beaten by Whites during a peaceful protest for the right to access beaches in Mississippi. Before Freedom Riders, Ruby Bridges, and lunch counter sit-ins, there had been wade-ins. This explains why my father never learned to swim.

I knew things weren't much better for Dad across the river in New Orleans. Not long after the family moved to Josephine Street when Dad was eleven, his older brother, Martin, was beaten up by a group of White sailors. Then, a Black man was beaten to death near his high school. Both incidents happened during Mardi Gras, near the French Quarter. "Mardi Gras was a dangerous time," he told me. "If you were Black you shouldn't be there in the Quarters." I only learned about these tragedies through my husband. Dad had told Dennis about it one day while they were having lunch together without me. I was newly pregnant with Dezi and meeting for the first time with both the family member who'd raped me and a therapist.

The news of Warren's lynching seemed to unlock a space in my father that had always been closed to me. For the first time, he shared with me about his childhood. He remembered a family trip to his mother's relatives on a run-down farm outside of Hattiesburg, Mississippi, and, on a separate occasion, visiting his uncle Clarence in the hospital. Clarence had been six feet two, with the loudest green eyes, and was an alcoholic. The family disease. "He was all cut up," Dad said, as if he'd been in a knife fight. Whatever happened to him had "something to do with drinking."

But these places were also where Dad went to dances, bought a car with a couple of friends, ate his own father's gumbo at Christmases, fished off the dock with his church's minister, went to see baseball games. Grandpa Martin was a catcher in the Negro Leagues in Mobile and Pascagoula, and told me he even had the chance to play against the famous pitcher Satchel Paige. Dad remembered that he and his brothers would go crabbing and bring their catches to the troop trains, where the Blacks, he said, always gave them more money than the Whites.

What a loss, to love a place and to fear it so deeply.

Even as an adult, Dad's uneasiness in the South was palpable. During our summer drives, first to Oklahoma and Arkansas, then down to New Orleans, we were always on guard. We knew better than to ask to stop for a bathroom break in Alabama or Mississippi, at least at night. We learned to hold it.

The threat of violence is also what made my great-grandfather on my mother's side leave Oklahoma. No one remembers how exactly my great-grandpa Sam Jones attracted the ire of the Klan in his small town. Mom thinks he may have killed a White man in self-defense. Whatever happened, Sam caught wind that the Klan was after him. So he faked dead and had himself nailed into a pine box, loaded onto a horse-drawn carriage, and wheeled out of town. He settled in Bakersfield, California, where my mom would spend a good part of her childhood before her father died and her mother remarried.

WHEN I WAS ARRESTED, I WAS ON SPRING BREAK FROM COLlege, visiting my best friend, Rachael, who was at Jacksonville University. We'd decided to spend a few days at Daytona. Rachael is White and so is her friend, who was driving. We were all drinking in the car, but I'm the one the motorcycle cop pointed to and told to get out. I was sitting in the back. I don't know how he'd seen me put the beer to my lips. The other girls had hidden their beers under their seats. I didn't mention that, of course. I didn't want them to get in trouble. And I would need them to bail me out.

The moto-cop handcuffed me right there on Daytona's main drag. At least I had on a cover-up over my bathing suit. Another girl, who'd also been pinched, was in just a bikini. We stood there for a while, moto-cop, bikini girl, and me, while he spoke into his walkie-talkie, waiting for pickup. Then he started chatting me up—Where was I from? Like it was a date. He told me I was the prettiest girl he'd handcuffed all night.

For the next six hours, bikini girl and I shared a makeshift cell for rowdy spring breakers that had been erected in the middle of a field.

She had the undefinable skin of my daughters. She kept coming on to the cops to try to get herself released and talking about all the ways she was going to fuck up her boyfriend when she got out. Somehow, her arrest was his fault. She wanted to know what I was doing in there, and I said I was drinking in a car, but I didn't want her to know that I was in college up north and on vacation with my friends. She was kind of scary. I had a feeling that would make her angry. She was still in the cell when my friend came to get me and I was now afraid for her.

The things we have to tell our children: Beware the police. Beware alcohol. Beware that one guy in our family, who seems nice and friendly. Your silence will hurt you. Being less Black, less hooded, less urban, less curvy, less, less, less is just another kind of silence. It will not save you. It will make you disappear completely.

I WISH I'D KNOWN ABOUT THE LYNCHING WHEN MONIQUE AND I
had gone down to Ocean Springs. Maybe we could have
paid Warren some kind of tribute, gone back to the bayou
where he was dragged and tossed a bouquet into its murky
waters, or found the persimmon tree where his body was
hung and put a plaque on the spot: "This tree bore strange
fruit. RIP Warren (Stuart) Mathews."

I wonder how Tempy could have continued to live in
that town for another twenty-four years until she died. I
wonder how any Black people functioned at all within the
constant terror cloaking the Deep South. And yet, in the
time I've lived in our idyllic suburb, three women, all Black,
have been killed by men they knew: Monica Paul was shot
by her ex at the family Y in front of her kids after a swim
class; Angela Bledsoe was shot by the father of her child too;
and Sarah Butler, who'd gone to school with Dezi, was strangled to death by someone she'd met online, her body left
in Eagle Rock Reservation, not far from the 9/11 memorial.

The Institute for Women's Policy Research reported
that Black women were two and a half times more likely to
be murdered by men than their White counterparts and
that more than nine in ten Black female victims knew their
killers.[2] Black women also experience significantly higher
rates of psychological abuse—including humiliation, in-
sults, name-calling, and coercive control—than do women
overall.

The newspaper articles about Warren's lynching sent
me into a deep funk. For about a week, the world shrunk to
my bed, the kitchen, the bus stop to drop off or pick up the

kids, the basement couch where I would lie until it was time to do it all again. Friends noticed. They grabbed at their hearts, or stroked my arm, or screwed up their faces in sympathy when I told them about Warren, and I felt both devastated and silly. Was I allowed to feel this way about the loss of someone I'd never met who'd died over a century ago?

Curled up on our basement couch, I clutched one of the pillows Monique had made for me, decorated with a decal of Tempy's Lost Friends ad. It reminded me of the pillow we passed to each other at survivors' group therapy.

When a friend from my book club told me that her husband's company was gathering information about lynching victims for a memorial in Alabama, I finally experienced something like relief. The Equal Justice Initiative memorial was years away from happening, but the idea that there would be a place to hold all that pain lifted something starting to settle in me. An adjacent terror has threaded through Black women's stories for centuries, apparent but unnamed. I never wanted to tell what had happened to me out of fear of being disloyal to my family, to my people. To tell was to feed the stereotype that Black men are sexual predators, a myth that got incalculable Black men lynched, including my great-granduncle.

"The institutionalized rape of black women has never been as powerful a symbol of black oppression as the spectacle of lynching," the African American studies scholar Hazel Carby writes.[3] Where was the monument to Black women's bodies assaulted, violated, controlled, patrolled since we were first forcibly brought here? When could we lay down a wreath to this war?

The same therapist who'd told me I had dissociated from my body, that I should try EMDR, said I was depressed. Oppressed, sure, historically. Repressed, probably. But depressed? That wasn't an option in my world. It had never been permitted in my vocabulary.

I had not even used the word on my twentieth birthday, when I almost didn't make it out of college alive. My two roommates had called my parents a few weeks before to say they were worried about me, that I was drinking too much and lashing out, sobbing uncontrollably. They were scared. My parents told me to pack some clothes. I would move home for the rest of the semester. They never asked me to stop drinking. And since I'd been behaving and it was my birthday, they agreed to let me spend the night in my dorm room.

I headed straight for the Lantern, a dive of a bar just outside of the campus gates. We Fordham Rams had a tradition: one free shot for every year you'd lived. I was twenty. I weighed 110 pounds. I lined up fifteen twinkling glasses in a row on the bar. The bartender wouldn't give me any more than that even though I kept reminding him of the ritual. In four-inch white heels with bows on the back, a light-pink dress that fit more like a body stocking, and big moussed hair, I climbed up on the slick knotted bar and demanded. I cursed at the bartender, but he would not budge. So I took off into the South Bronx night, down Fordham Road, alone. I walked for a half mile, past Korean nail salons, the old Abraham & Strauss, and a check-cashing store toward the school's tallest spire, my landmark. Just outside of the campus gates, I lost steam. I could see my dorm room window now, but I couldn't make my body move. I sat down right above a sewer drain to collect myself.

Someone stopped in the street to ask after me. "Are you a student here?" I think I nodded. I don't remember if I could still speak.

"Then you should go inside the gates. You look homeless."

Homeless. How I feel when people say I'm not really Black. How I will feel when I first try to tell my mother about the rapes and she puts her hands over her ears and yells, "I can't hear this."

I remember getting to my loft, feeling pathetic and alone. I remember swallowing a bunch of pills. I don't remember noticing that anyone else was in the room, but then someone was asking from below, "What did you take? What did you do?" I remember the ambulance, but I don't remember riding in it. I remember my parents' twisted faces, churning with anger when they came to get me. For two more years I kept on drinking, not sure whether to live or die.

A FEW WEEKS AFTER DAD AND I TALKED, I WENT TO A VIRGINIA artists' colony to begin this book about my family's history. Despite myself, and after all I had learned, I questioned my work's relevance. I was married to a White man in a multiracial town. I was at an artists' colony down the street from a former plantation that had been converted into a women's college that was working hard to preserve the history of the enslaved community that once lived there. I went for a run wondering if maybe all of this history was just dead weight. I upped my pace as I turned the corner, sped past a literal junkyard dog, and headed up the hill that led to the busy main road. That's when I saw out of the corner of my eye a swastika flying on a pole in someone's front yard. I looked again, worried that I was having some kind of post-traumatic stress vision. But the swastika kept waving at me in the late November breeze. Except for the barking dog, I was alone. When I finally turned onto the residency's gravel road, I felt a violent clamp on my intestines, like someone had put them in a vise, and humbly came to understand what it means when people say, "I nearly had the shit scared out of me."

CHAPTER 17
MEETING THE STUARTS

A few days after the swastika sighting, I drove out of the Blue Ridge Mountains toward the sea to pay a visit to the Colonel's portrait. It was in the home of Elizabeth Monrose Lacouture, William Hill Howcott's granddaughter and Lizzie's distant cousin, in Virginia Beach, about a four-hour drive from the artist's colony.

When she opened the door, she reminded me of my mother. Not just because they shared a name, Betty, but because of the way she carried herself. Betty had a daytime layer of foundation on her face, ivory white with a splash of pink across the lips that matched her sweater. My mom would have received a stranger on a Thursday afternoon the same way. Betty also had curled her thinning white hair under at the ends. Back in the day, my mom would have put on a wig.

Betty offered me a drink, then brought me right to the living room. The Colonel's portrait was above her fireplace, guarded by two sculpted ducks on the mantel. There was no life in his gray eyes, no warmth, no intensity to his expression. Even his hair was noncommittal, a bit reddish, not red proper like Dennis's. I could barely focus on him. The artist, G. P. A. Healy, was considered the most successful portrait painter of his time and known for capturing his subject's likeness. I wondered if the Colonel and everyone he knew had seen him as removed.

My eyes wandered from his grim sagging jowls and black overcoat to the ornate wooden frame he was bound in, then to his caretaker, paces away in the kitchen, artfully arranging the fall bouquet I'd brought her like it might be exhibited in a museum, her museum.

We discussed my drive, what all we'd be doing for Thanksgiving the following week (she was hosting, like my mom), our children, everything but the painting. The Colonel seemed just a mutual acquaintance, the person who had introduced us, and was not ultimately the center of our attention. Betty took a picture of me with him then gestured at the room, which was filled with portraits, books, and family photos. "I really live here," she said. It made good sense for Colonel Stuart's portrait to overlook the center of the house. From the Old English *stig* for "house(hold)" and *weard* for "guardian," Stuarts are the guardians of the home.

BIG WILL'S PORTRAIT WAS IN THE BASEMENT OF THE MARYLAND Historical Society, the same place Dana ends up at the end of *Kindred*. A few blocks away, my husband's niece was studying art, so she came with me to see him on my way to the artists' retreat. Great-great-great-grandpa was on the bottom row at the end of a rack of stored paintings. The wooden hand-painted frame was chipped in one place and the 150-year-old portrait cracked throughout. William Stuart's eyes had a translucent quality and he wore a thinly veiled smile. He looked the way he sounded in his letters: indignant, self-righteous, thoughtful.

What would Big Will have thought of me, I wondered, a Black woman, paying such a pilgrimage to his likeness? From what I've read of his letters, he'd probably be less anxious about the color of my skin and our relationship to each other than the fact that they were keeping him in the basement. What a reflection of how his life ended: moneyless, jobless, homeless, and squatting at his son's house. At least he wasn't alone. His sons Charles and Alexander, and Alexander's wife, adorned in glasses and an ermine robe, were all in the same basement. These were the portraits that had once hung in the Colonel and Elizabeth's parlor in Ocean Springs, mentioned in Elizabeth's will.

"My Dear Sir, Your two last letters came safe to hand the last one accompanied by Mark who I sold to Mr. John Wriggly for Two hundred dollars. . . . He was quite small for his age. Had he been the ordinary size I could have got at least 225 $ for him. Your wheat sold for 95 cts. The rye

35."[1] The Colonel's father, Big Will, a Maryland merchant, wrote this letter to one of his customers.

I hadn't expected that Big Will sold slaves since he'd advised his sons "not to get involved in slavery." (The Colonel's brother, Alexander, didn't listen to his father either. He was selling slaves in Natchez, Mississippi.) Maybe all of Big Will's religious fervor was the result of a conversion in thought. He never articulated any remorse in his letters, but I sensed him struggling with something on the page.

I read through Big Will's letters at the archive at Washington College, in Kent County, just across the Chesapeake Bay from Baltimore. He was morally suspect, hypocritical, overbearing, but there was a sincere longing in him that I recognized. I could hear it in his letters. I could see it in his painting.

One of the letters I came across was from Big Will to the Colonel from Canton, Mississippi, in April 1850. Big Will was visiting his daughter, Susan Handy, and it seems likely that the Colonel, who was only sixty miles away in Baton Rouge, would have gone to Canton to see his father and sister. The exchange made me wonder if Susan had perhaps entertained the Colonel and her neighbors, the McCauleys. Perhaps she would have introduced her brother to his future wife, Elizabeth, then nine years old, and her twenty-nine-year-old nurse and slave, Tempy.

Some White families arranged "concubinage relationships" as incentives to marry. Brenda Stevenson's essay "What's Love Got to Do with It?" describes one such case. John Sella Martin's father, a White man of "limited financial

means," was meant to marry someone with substantial property—his family had arranged it—but the bride-to-be was
much younger than he was. "It would be at least a decade
before she was ready to marry," Stevenson writes. The man's
aunt persuaded him to wait to marry the heiress by arranging a "concubinage relationship" with an enslaved woman,
Winnifred, who then gave birth to John. "Winnifred was
Mr. Martin's concubine for the next ten years," and, ultimately, when it came time to marry, Mr. Martin refused. He
was too attached to his enslaved family.

Concubinage relationships ran the gamut from brutal
assaults to mimicking marriages. "Most enslaved women
quickly learned that to resist these sexual demands meant
some sort of punishment," Stevenson writes. "Still, the reactions of enslaved women who were pursued by slaveholding
men for sexual favor varied substantially." Some committed
suicide, others murdered their assailants. They tried to escape or begged to be sold; some resigned themselves to lives
of sexual slavery and carried the scars throughout their lives.
Some "came to appreciate the material benefits and prom-
ises of freedom" they received in exchange. Stevenson found
most evidence of "sexual compliance" in Louisiana. The
story of slavery is the story of Black women and their bodies.

Elizabeth's body was not a powerful thing, but Tempy's
was by all accounts. The Colonel would have had dominion
over them both, as well as any of the children. "Increase,"
the word for unborn enslaved children; "breeder," the term
for an enslaved woman with many childbearing years ahead
of her; "fancy girl," a sexual slave.

BETTY WOULD TELL ME THAT SHE HOPED THAT THERE WAS some genuine emotion between the Colonel and Tempy, and that she hoped that hope wasn't naive. I remembered myself in the cavernous stale dining room in New York City with the reporter from the "Love vs. Bigotry" article, hoping the same thing.

I also spoke to Peter Monrose, Betty's brother. We talked, first, about Willis, who, Peter told me, had simply served his master, not the Confederacy, the way Black Confederate theorists believe. Years later, it seems, when Peter's grandfather, William Hill Howcott, erected the monument to Willis, he made sure it was slightly taller than the other Confederate monuments, because he was angry the town wouldn't let him place it inside the Confederate cemetery. After that, William Hill was run out of town.

Peter was about seven when he traveled the eighty miles from his home in Waveland, Mississippi, to Ocean Springs to visit with his elderly cousin, Lizzie. That was when he met Tempy, he said. She must have been close to one hundred years old then. I wanted to know everything: Was her voice low or high? Did she have a way of laughing, holding her head? What was she wearing? Did she seem happy? But Peter was close to one hundred himself by the time of our phone conversation. All he could remember was a distant flash of my great-great-grandmother getting butter from the yard. That was something. After a century of living, she could still carry her own weight.

I could still taste the butter we made in kindergarten at the Little Red School House—creamy, a little bit salty and sweet. I could see my father, who made ice cream when he was a boy in Ocean Springs, sitting on the frozen treat until his butt went numb, and my children making ice cream in our backyard in some contraption that they rolled on the ground between themselves. Peter's memory sparked my own, and my father's, and my children's, creating a circle that began with Tempy, made her spirit materialize. I couldn't believe I was talking to someone who'd spoken to her, breathed in the same air. The past never dies. We are never that separate from it. We'd threaded the needle of time.

"She had a son, Alfred. I met him too. All I knew was that one of Aunt Tempy's sons had been lynched. I knew that. What I heard was a group of men came over from Biloxi."

I asked him if he knew why the men had come to lynch Tempy's son, but he said no.

"I heard that on the way home the boat overturned and some of the men drowned." Apparently Peter had overheard Tempy say this while listening in on the grown-ups.

The weather in Back Bay of Biloxi, where the men who lynched Uncle Warren landed, was foul on the night of February 1, 1901. The crowd must have slipped and sunk in the muddy ground as they dragged Warren along. I imagined Warren's family, trekking into the wooded area after everyone was gone, howling and praying, then slipping an egg into his hand before retrieving his lifeless body. "A fresh egg in the hand of a murder victim will prevent the murderer's going far from the scene," Zora Neale Hurston wrote in her collection of Black folklore *Mules and Men.* "The egg represents life, and so the dead victim is holding the life of the murderer in his hand." The Colonel, volunteer Confederate soldier, guardian of the home, was no longer alive and could not protect his son. It was left to the place, to Mother Nature, to get the final job of justice done.

I am with the portrait of my third great-grandfather
"Big Will" at the Maryland Historical Society
(photo by Flannery Silva).

CHAPTER 18

COMING TO THE TABLE

"We do not pray to have more money. We pray for
more kinsmen."

—Chinua Achebe

SYLVIA HAD NEVER HEARD OF THE FORDS, BUT SHE HAD HEARD
about the lynching of her "grandfather's little brother"
when she was a young woman in the sixties. Her father had
told her. Alfred Burton Stuart was Sylvia's great-grandfather.
Tempy Elizabeth, the musical cousin, was her grandmother.
Sylvia lived in New York City, had a media background, and
was also researching her family's history. At the close of 2010,
Monique found her on Ancestry. Elegant, no-nonsense, and

funny, Sylvia acted the way Josephine's editorials sounded. Maybe they both got it from Alfred.

Alfred was known to walk around town with his shirt open and his chest out. According to local genealogies and his obituary, he was confident, respected, and well-liked by folks across the color line.[1] He made his living as a truck farmer, selling the vegetables he raised. Around the same time that Tempy became a property owner, Alfred opened a dairy. During planting season for melons and sweet potatoes and harvesting for okra and peas, in May 1892, Alfred and his father, the Colonel, registered to vote on the same day. A presidential election and the town's first mayoral race loomed. I've wondered if, to begin that dairy, Alfred received some kind of loan or gift from the Colonel. The idea is less far-fetched than Alfred and his White father/ former master registering to vote in Mississippi together. It's less far-fetched than Alfred being able to register at all. In the years after emancipation, 90 percent of voting-age Black men were registered to vote in Mississippi. By 1892, the number was slashed to less than 6 percent. Alfred and Ocean Springs were some kind of Mississippi anomaly.

In 1881, Alfred married Clara Harding in Saint Mary's Parish, the same place where, decades earlier, Tempy had been separated from her family. One of the largest slaveholders in the parish was Winthrop Sargent Harding; in 1860, his estate had 124 slaves. Winthrop married into a powerful plantation family, the Conrads, and his wife's nephew married Mary Stirling, cousin to Dr. Ruffin Grey Stirling. So the Hardings were also Dr. Stirling's people.

Maybe Alfred was sent to Saint Mary on a mission to find his mother's people and came back with a wife instead. He was twenty years old by then, the man of the family. Maybe he sent himself.

Back in Ocean Springs, Alfred became one of the "colored" school's trustees. The town's first school for Black children was erected in 1909. The year before, perhaps influenced by Alfred, Josephine sent her oldest child and only daughter, Rosa Bell, to private school in New Orleans; she entered Straight University as a seventh grader in 1908 and graduated from its preparatory school in 1915. A historically Black college started in 1869 through the Methodist Church's Freedman's Aid Society, Straight later merged with New Orleans University and was renamed Dillard. Gilbert Academy was a unit of New Orleans University, so in essence my father attended his aunt's alma mater without knowing it. Sylvia had come across Rosa Bell's school yearbook at the Amistad Research Center in New Orleans.

The pain of the lynching still preoccupied my newfound cousin. Even though Tempy Elizabeth had been a witness to the horror, according to other relatives, she had never talked about it. No one in the family had. At our cousins get-together we alternated between guttural laughter and tears over this shared past. Monique gave Sylvia copies of the articles about it and I told her about Coming to the Table and its upcoming National Gathering in Richmond. CTTT's approach is based on the Strategies for Trauma Awareness and Resilience program that began in response to the 9/11 attacks. It combines theory and practices from neurobiology, conflict transformation, spirituality, and restorative justice to address the needs of trauma-impacted individuals and communities. Sylvia joined CTTT the day after we met and decided to attend the gathering too.

The event was held in Richmond over a weekend and featured guest speakers and workshops on everything from identifying and preserving enslaved burial grounds to how to approach linked descendants, people connected to one another through slavery and its legacies. Howard Zehr, considered father of the restorative justice movement in the United States, led a workshop focused on an approach he'd observed among the Indigenous of the South Pacific: community, not the legal system, takes the lead in identifying the harm done and the best way for the perpetrator to fix it.

He asked us, What brought you to this workshop? What would justice or reparation look like to you? Are there any stakeholders you can involve to help move toward repair?

I told our small group about the Howcott/Stuart property and my great-granduncle Warren. I wasn't sure what reparations could look like in terms of the property, but when it came to Warren, the center of Ocean Springs popped into my mind, the quaint shops, the trolley car, the City of Discovery sign, and a sapling, no taller than my children. That's what I wanted, an acknowledgment of what had happened to Warren that would be alive and near permanent, growing as my girls grew, where I could go, take cover, or reflect, with a bronze plate fixed to it or words etched in granite at its base. That would give this place back to my family. The kind staff and members at Saint Paul's

Methodist Church, the folks at Saint James, the ladies at the Jackson County Archives, the Find a Grave volunteer, my cousins Sylvia and Monique could all have a stake in it too.

Our gathering site, Richmond Hill, was an ecumenical community atop the highest point in the city, capital of the Confederacy. "I could feel the angels and devils there," Sylvia said.[2] It overlooked the James River and what used to be the second largest slave-trading post in the country. I went out to the gardens after the Zehr workshop to collect myself. Maybe I walked the labyrinth. Maybe I made circles in the gravel with my toe. Those simple steps, hearing myself identify harm and desire, had unleashed a wave of harm and desire in me.

When lunchtime came, I was ready to talk about anything else, even DNA, a popular topic. Everyone was asking:

Have you done it?

Did you use Ancestry or 23andMe?

But do you trust it?

By the time of the gathering, in March 2012, genetic ancestry testing was ubiquitous, and for many it repaired a narrative ruptured by slavery. I had mixed feelings. I had taken a DNA test recently, offered for free as a way of getting more African American samples; I was eager to know if we were Yoruba, like the last survivor of the middle passage to the United States, or if we came from Ghana, home of the Akan people, where lineage is traced through the mother and maternal ancestors. It was the work of the Howard University geneticists who had identified the fifteen thousand enslaved folk in the colonial burial ground a stone's throw from Wall Street that had led to advances in consumer DNA testing and the African Ancestry testing company.

But I was hoping for something more substantial or maybe spiritual than spitting in a vial or sticking a Q-tip into my cheek. I wanted something like *The Language You Cry In*. In that documentary, a Gullah woman in Georgia discovers her ancestral home in Sierra Leone through a song her mother used to sing to her.

"DNA can offer an avenue toward recognition, but cannot stand in for reconciliation," Dr. Alondra Nelson writes in *The Social Life of DNA: Race, Reparations, and Reconciliation After the Genome*. To Nelson, reparations is voice, acknowledgment, mourning, forgiveness, healing. It's beyond the scope of science, and double-edged.

DNA exonerated the wrongly accused Central Park Five and convicted the Golden State killer, who eluded authorities for decades. If it weren't for the DNA evidence that concluded Thomas Jefferson fathered at least one child with Sally Hemings, the Black and White Jefferson descendants would not have been invited on *Oprah*, might never have met, and there might not be a Coming to the Table. After the show, descendants from both branches of the family got to know each other and gathered together at Monticello, inspiring one of the White cousins to co-found the organization. But science has also been used to exploit Black people like the men who participated in the Tuskegee experiment and Henrietta Lacks, whose genetic material was used without her consent. At the gathering, a woman in our lunch crew and her father decided that he would be the one in the family to test his DNA because, at his age, he would be the least vulnerable if his results were misused.

"In looking at the uses and abuses of genetic claims, one can only conclude that DNA is Janus-faced," Nelson writes. "Yet with genetic ancestry testing, these two ways of looking are also sankofa." Sankofa. It can mean to go back and get it and it can also mean justice.

WHEN BOTH MY CHILDREN STARTED SCHOOL, I BEGAN TO THINK about filing charges against my abuser—not because I wanted him to go to jail, but because I thought it could force him to get help, ensure he wouldn't hurt anyone else, and pay for my mounting therapy fees. But there is a limit on how long you can wait from the time of injury to file charges, and it had passed. Some people think the same about reparations: that it's been too long.

Harriet Tubman had to wait thirty-four years for any compensation for her work for the Union, finally receiving a widow's pension for her husband's service. The Ex-Slave Mutual Relief, Bounty, and Pension Association lobbied for a pension for the formerly enslaved similar to what Union soldiers received. Congress never took it seriously. Instead, the government charged the association's most prominent leaders with mail fraud.

Queen Mother Audley Moore, the granddaughter of captives in Louisiana, gathered a million signatures on a petition demanding reparations and presented it to

President John F. Kennedy on the eve of the centennial of the Emancipation Proclamation. She passed the baton to the National Coalition of Blacks for Reparations in America (N'COBRA), which formed in 1987. Deadria Farmer-Paellmann, a longtime activist for reparations and onetime law clerk for N'COBRA, led a twenty-six-hour drum vigil to bring attention to and protest the dispossession of the Africans buried in lower Manhattan. Visiting the African Burial Ground, that colonial graveyard, inspired her to go to law school and seek reparations by suing big brokerage companies involved in slavery. Her lawyers used DNA linking the claimants to Africa in their arguments. "Our injury," Farmer-Paellmann said, "is that we don't know who we are."[3]

When he ran for president in 1988, Jesse Jackson's platform included reparations for descendants of the enslaved along with single payer/universal health care and a WPA-style program to put all Americans to work. I, personally, would like to see WPA-style reparations along the lines of the digitization of privately held records on slavery, which could be made public through a government-funded program, and the increasing accessibility of slavery insurance policies from firms like Aetna, New York Life, and Lloyd's of London. An insurance policy at Lloyd's of London, for instance, was the key to Alex Haley finding his ancestor Kunta Kinte. The cases that Farmer-Paellmann filed were dismissed, but Lloyd's of London did apologize for its role in financing slavery and its connection to the slave trade, announcing that it would make reparations.

In the early 2000s, California adopted legislation requiring insurance companies with any documentation of slavery-era insurance policies to make their records available, and about a dozen states followed suit. Now, California is leading the way in reparations as the first state to create a task force and pay for beachfront property unjustly seized from a Black family. Perhaps other states will follow on this too.

Woullard Lett, a member of N'COBRA who is also a UU, describes reparations as a human covenant, "the midpoint between truth and reconciliation."[4]

That's where I am all these years later, in the middle.

Telling was the beginning. After I told God, and the survivors' group, and a boyfriend who responded that he was sorry to hear it but more worried about my drinking, I went to AA and told the women there. Then I told my sister, because she was worried about how distant I'd been from our family.

I'd like to be able to say that I told the rest of my family because I'd found clarity and courage, believed it was not my fault, that my particular pain did not need to be quantified in order to hold those who had caused it to account. But I told my family because I was afraid it would happen again.

I was working part-time at a newspaper on the cop desk, calling the police all over our county to find out if anything interesting had happened that day. During one of my shifts, my sister called with concerns. "So, [our relative] has been 'visiting' our niece while her parents are at work." I could hear the quotation marks around the word "visiting." I could hear the strain in her voice above the steady din in the newsroom. I was twenty-two, fresh out of college, newly sober, emerging. I decided to tell my other family members in letters, not unlike the ones Josephine wrote to Uncle Cephas.

That way, I would not have to bear witness to everyone's reactions. I would not have to watch if my parents died on the spot. But my mother did not die. Instead, she called me up. Her voice sounded light.

"Hey D-bug. We got your letter," she said. She wanted to meet with my therapist and me. She said she was sorry about what had happened. She told me she loved me. I felt so close to her after I broke my silence, like a real part of my family, like I belonged. But abuse and betrayal, breach of the body, are relentless beasts, deeply rooted, soul-choking weeds. Years later, when I didn't want to go to my perpetrator's wedding, my mother screamed into the phone at me before hanging up in my face. "You're so selfish," she said. "What will her family think?" I was too nauseous from early pregnancy to scream back or cry. To stop my stomach from roiling, I laid out on the bed in our apartment and looked out the window above Third Avenue, resigning myself to the fact that the new family I was making would be my only family.

Days after that, through an appointment arranged by my dad, I sat in a different therapist's office with my abuser, and for the first time he admitted what he'd done more than twenty years before. Some people say, "Forgive and forget." I say, "Remember and recover." *Re-member. Put yourself back together again and again.*

CHAPTER 19

MONUMENTS

The town where Willis once lived had a left-behind feeling to it, like an abandoned movie set. Real movies were filmed there—*A Time to Kill, My Dog Skip*—and live music was broadcast from old-timey metal speakers suspended from high perches across from the courthouse on the square. Confederate flags were everywhere, flying from the statehouse building, flapping above the oak double doors of the inn where I was staying with all of William Hill's descendants.

Canton is in Madison County, Mississippi, where the first broadly publicized lynching occurred and, as civil rights activist Anne Moody writes in her autobiography, "where Negroes frequently turned up dead."[1] While a student at

Tougaloo College, Moody joined the Congress of Racial Equality. A month before the March on Washington, CORE opened an office in Canton to start a voter-registration campaign, and Moody decided to work there. "Shortly before Christmas a man's headless corpse had been found on the road between Canton and Tougaloo with the genitals cut off and with K's cut into the flesh all over his body," she writes. Her friends and her mentor, Reverend Ed King, all tried to talk her out of going. But she was resolved. Black people outnumbered Whites three to one and owned over 40 percent of the land in the county, and yet there were only about 150 registered to vote out of tens of thousands.

As for me, I was ready to leave as soon as I pulled into the driveway. The Stars and Bars everywhere I looked were getting to me. But I felt I owed Willis my presence. Thirteen. Just a boy when he was sent off to help his captors with their war. So I stayed through crab cakes that night, grits and gravy the next morning, and three generations of Howcotts, their family story rolling off their tongues like butter down the sides of hot biscuits.

On the drive from the inn to the ceremony, one of William Hill's great-granddaughters asked me what I thought about reparations. Something about her hair made me think of Scout Finch from the *To Kill a Mockingbird* movie. I answered with a question: "What do you think of them? How would you feel if someone like me came looking for them?" She said she had an idea for an education pool that people could contribute to based on how much they had benefited from slavery, but did not believe her family necessarily owed reparations to anybody. Another great-granddaughter was worried that no one in her family had reached out to the mostly Black community about the monument being moved from their neighborhood to the Canton Historical Society, not far from the Confederate cemetery.

I wondered how the monument would be represented by a historical society that had deep ties to the Daughters of the Confederacy. And I worried about my presence there, that it might be taken as an endorsement. I thought of Ida B. Wells, grappling with whether to attend the Columbian Exposition of 1893. *If we go, the White people think we're satisfied with our one-day allotment. If we don't go, they conclude we have no innovation to offer the country.* Ida sat outside and handed out slips of paper explaining how she was there but not there, in it but not of it.

At the end of the ceremony, during the benediction, the Daughters tried to claim that Willis had served the Confederacy. But William Hill's great-granddaughter Joan told the truth in her speech: that he was an enslaved boy holding his enslaver's horse on the battlefield.

Eventually, Moody's work in Canton caught the attention of the Klan and she ended up on a blacklist along with Medgar Evers and James Meredith. She tried to shake off the fear with some time in the woods, her "cure," but back in Canton she realized she had not been cured. She began to feel "choked up again." "More than ever, I began to wonder whether God actually existed. Maybe God changed as the individual changed or grew as one grew." At work on the Freedom Vote, she felt like a robot, like her feet were weighed down by irons, and she could barely think. She decided to take a break from the movement.

I still can't explain why I went to Canton, what it was I felt I owed to Willis by being there. Sometimes all of these traumas collide, like the repeating names in enslaving families and the mirrored names given to the people they enslaved, and I can't keep track of what I'm responding to, then or now, or where I'm going.

Willis was family. The Colonel was family.

I WAS LOOKING FOR SOMETHING IN THE COLONEL TO REDEEM him, to reconcile myself to him as a part of my family, because that's what I've always done. Because family is family, a monument. The only reason my abuser had come to see the therapist with me that day is so that I would attend his wedding. My absence would have been tricky to explain to his bride. In the therapist's office, he admitted what he'd done, but he did not say sorry. And he hasn't said sorry since.

What I most regret is how this perpetration has stolen intimacy from me, robbed me of time with the people I most want to love, including my perpetrator, whom I had been so close to. I blame it for every spoiled relationship. I cannot begin to calculate how much I have paid to treat myself for abuse at the hands of my relative and the hands of my country. I have disowned my own body. I have spent countless dollars. No therapeutic treatment I have ever sought has been covered by my insurance. According to the results of the Adverse Childhood Experiences study, child abuse is the gravest and most costly public health issue in the United States.[2] A principal creator of the study believes that eradicating childhood abuse in America would reduce depression by more than half, alcoholism by two-thirds, and suicide and domestic violence by three-quarters.

Confederate statues are coming down all over the country, and I'm sure that someone will be coming for Willis's soon. But erasure is not the same as repair, and I'm afraid that if Willis's statue is gone, in time, no one will believe the things this country did except those of us who carry the epigenetic memory and can commune with our dead.

EPILOGUE
ALTARS

North is water, healing. South is fire, ancestral. I pour water on the rosemary plant outside of my kitchen every morning, say hello to my grandmothers and my grandfathers, then light a candle and sit down with them before I head out into the world.

No question to my grandmothers goes unanswered. No grandfather goes unacknowledged. For years, I kept the picture of my Burton and Stuart ancestors on my altar, the picture folded over so I didn't have to see the Colonel's face. But one day, I was at an ancestral retreat and a woman asked our elder what to do with the ancestors who have hurt us or were just terrible people. "Do we leave them off of our altar?" Our elder said no, to include them too. They more than anyone want to help us, they need to help us to try to make things right from the other side. I still wasn't sure, but I gave it a try, unfolded the picture so the whole truth of my family was there on my altar in black and white. When I stepped outside on the patio of the retreat house, there was a hummingbird, feeding. It's the only bird that can fly backward, exploring the past as it draws from it "the nectars of joy," a real life sankofa.[1]

I make sure to look at the Colonel's face when I greet my other grandfathers too.

I leave them flowers and pecans. They press into my emptiness.

At the end of this spiritual cycle, seven years after I hovered over myself in the shower, I cut the chemicals from my hair, took my family to Brazil, and went to Hilton Head, where my daughters had first learned how to ride bikes on the wide expanse of hard-packed sand and Devany swam underwater for the first time. My grandparents, former sharecroppers, who went back to school in their fifties so they could get their GEDs, bought a timeshare in Hilton Head on spec in the eighties, at the beginning of the development boom. Land and literacy were their primary concerns, like so many Southern Black people of their generation. They are a part of my altar now.

My White Stuart cousin happened to be vacationing at Hilton Head at the same time. She and her sister had led us to the portrait of our common ancestor, Alexander Stuart, in the Baltimore Museum of Art and to documents about his Revolutionary War service. I wore long pants to our lunch together even though it was sweltering, to hide my bandages. I'd been stung by a Portuguese man-of-war and the blisters on my shins grew so big I had to wrap them up and drag them around with me. In the picture this cousin's husband took of us, you cannot tell that I'm in pain. My cousin and I look almost similar with our wide-eyed smiles and short haircuts.

I'd fallen down the ancestry rabbit hole and was climbing my way out.

On the drive to the beach from New Jersey, the car full of boogie boards and sand pails, we passed a sign for Burton, North Carolina, and I asked myself, once again, if the Burtons were my family. Are my family. In Brazil we had gone to see a Confederate monument where, on each side of the rebel flag, a list appeared of the town's Americans. At the top of the second row was the name Burton.

In a database of emancipation petitions, I found that a man named Allen Burton in Lauderdale County, Alabama, had tried to free his slaves in his will, however strangely. Four names of the people he'd enslaved matched with my family: Tempy, Polly, Nancy, and Albert.[2]

He wrote:

> It is my will and desire that my nephews Lewis & Oscar shall enjoy the use and benefit of the services of all my negroes which may remain after my decease for the term of five years from the day of my death equally and at the expiration of that time, it is my will that they all be transported to the state of Ohio by my said nephews, Lewis & Oscar for the

purpose of emancipating them from bondage according to the laws of that state and then the said Lewis and Oscar whom I will appoint my executors or either of them shall provide for them by purchase two hundred acres of tillable land and furnish them with such stock and utensils as may be necessary for their comfortable settlement the title to the aforesaid land to be held in the name of my executor for the use and benefit of the slaves which I hereby intend to liberate.

This was the sixth of many decrees in Allen Burton's will. If he is the right Burton, this might explain why Tempy, her mother, and some siblings kept the Burton name. Burton, their first enslaver, intended to give them their freedom.

But the executors of Allen Burton's estate told the court "that from the number and ages of the slaves and the great number of shares into which they are required to be divided, that distribution cannot be made of them in any kind, fairly equally & beneficially among the parties entitled thereto." Instead, they proposed "that your Honor will grant them an order to make sale of said slaves," then split the proceeds. Their request was granted.

We could have been freer, sooner. Maybe.

MY FAMILY VISITED THE NATIONAL MUSEUM OF AFRICAN American History and Culture not long after it opened its doors, just before Dezi left to college.

*Five generations of women in my family on Hilton Head,
South Carolina. The youngest is my grandniece, Selena, being held
by her mom, my niece Shaunte. The oldest is our matriarch,
my grandmother Louise, in the middle.*

We walked through a doorway into a darkened, cramped
space, a replica of a Portuguese slave ship that wrecked
on its way to Brazil. Sexual violence began for the women
aboard these ships, crossing the Atlantic. "Buryed a girl slave
(No 92)," John Newton, who was a slave trader before he
composed "Amazing Grace," wrote in June 1754.

"In the afternoon while we were off the deck, William
Cooney seduced a woman slave down into the room and
lay with her brutelike in view of the whole quarter deck, for

Dennis, Desiree, me, and Devany in front of Igreja do Senhor do Bonfim, Salvador, Bahia.

which I put him in irons. l hope this has been the first affair of the kind on board and I am determined to keep them quiet if possible. If anything happens to the woman I shall impute it to him, for she was big with child. Her number is 83."[3]

Our daughters went to see Chuck Berry's Cadillac while Dennis and I wandered through the floor on Jim Crow and the civil rights movement.

"This is overwhelming. I need to get to the hope," I overheard another Black woman in the exhibit say, as she walked toward me. "Me too," I said, even though she wasn't talking to me. I'd just seen the installation memorializing the murders of civil rights activists, including Unitarian Universalists, and noticed rows of rectangular plaques beneath. As I crossed paths with the woman, I understood what the plaques were; the names of lynching victims were etched into frosted glass. They were scattered around the floor but not in any particular order that I could discern. There had to be thousands of them. There were even more underneath the "Hardening of Racial Separation" gallery. I stopped and scanned the rows. One of the plaques bore my great-granduncle Warren's name.

I bent down next to the tag, this national acknowledgment of a century-old, very public family tragedy, in a museum that was a hundred years in the making. It took the wind out of me; I couldn't get up. When Dennis found me there, crouched down and bewildered, he asked me what the matter was. All I could say was, "Uncle. Uncle."

I don't have any more uncles—Martin, Henry, Walter all are gone. We used to cry uncle when we couldn't take any more tickling, or pummeling. Uncle. Uncle. Surrender.

MY SEVENTEEN-YEAR-OLD TOLD ME THAT SHE'D BEEN AS-saulted three years before by an acquaintance. It was a few months into the COVID pandemic and a few months before the country's first permanent memorial to survivors of sexual assault would be installed in Minneapolis. She told me in the kitchen, where all of the most important things in our family have happened and where a macaroni necklace, multicolored like the one my grandpa placed around my neck when I was twelve, hangs from the corkboard like a rosary. We put so much energy into teaching potential victims how not to be victimized but not enough into teaching potential predators how not to prey.

One of the lasting effects of the childhood violence I experienced is that the present and past collide sometimes. When this happens, my mind tries to leave my body. But I did everything I could to remain in the kitchen with her. I remembered her: her first visit to the Hayden Planetarium, us under a canopy of stars watching a reenactment of the cosmic collision that was the beginning of everything and the star dust, left behind, that lives in all of us; us marching with our capoeira academy in the town's Fourth of July parade and then me carrying her the rest of the way; the prayers we tied to the gate of a half Catholic, half Candomblé church in Bahia. *In every lonely place I found an altar.*

I struggled to stay connected. Connected, the opposite of addicted. How do I do this, remain alert and in my body while raising these young women, trying to protect them and failing, trying to model for them when to march, when to rest, when to look and when to look away?

We decided we needed to fly. So we went out to the trampoline that Dennis in all his wisdom had bought at the beginning of the pandemic. We could see the top of the magnolia, Mississippi's state flower, so much like an ipê tree. Bouncing ourselves breathless, up into the branches, I felt that energy running through me like I sometimes do when I meditate. I felt that clarity of my time on the plane when I thought I was about to die and knew my relationship to God needed to change. I thought of all the Black women in our town who'd been killed by men who professed adoration for them and felt the distance between God and me, my daughter and me, my mind and my body, closing.

If you go looking for your enslaved ancestors, you will learn your history so well that you'll stop having to look for it. Putting it behind you would be as impossible a task as living without your head. Because it's in you, as close as your breath. It is your essence. It is you, embodied. It is your blessing. You are a blessing. May it be so. Ase.

ACKNOWLEDGMENTS

I've wanted to tell the stories of my great-great-grandparents since I first heard about them when I was twelve. Without my family's stories, this book wouldn't be possible. To my grandparents, Martin Ford, Lillie Mae Ford, Louise Walton, and Alonzo Walton; my parents, Joseph and Betty Ford; my uncle Henry Ford; my cousin Shawnique Ford Rixner; my sister Diana Penn; and to the extended family I met along the way, especially Monique Smith Andersen and Sylvia Wong Lewis—thank you for sharing your stories with me.

It was an immense communal effort to bring this book into the world and I am extremely grateful for, indebted to, and also thank the following:

Duvall Osteen believed in this book before it was a full book—thank you for taking me on as a client and finding a perfect home for my work.

The brilliant Hillary Brenhouse engaged in a deep conversation with me about my life and my family's history. Thank you for asking questions that I had not asked myself that give this book the shape it needed. Thank you to Claire Zuo, Lindsay Fradkoff, Jocelynn Pedro, Shena Redmond, Clive Priddle, and the entire Bold Type team for your care and stewardship. Fact checking by Alexander Johnson and copy editing by Liz Dana made this a better book and the stellar cover by Pete Garceau far exceeded my hopes.

The Virginia Center for the Creative Arts, Hedgebrook, MacDowell, Yaddo, Martha MOCA, and The Cabins fed, housed, and supplied me with friendship, kinship, and sustaining company. Thank you for the gift of time and space to work among other artists.

The National Endowment for the Arts, the Sustainable Arts Foundation, and Louisiana State University Libraries Special Collections Research Grant provided much appreciated and needed financial support that allowed me to keep researching and writing and buoyed my confidence.

Brain, Child, LitHub, TueNight, and *More* magazines published articles that were the root of this book and I especially thank Nanette Varian for editing the essay that led to awards from the National Association of Black Journalists and the Newswomen's Club of New York.

The following institutions archived information necessary for my research, and their staffs were all extremely helpful and patient: The Mississippi State University Libraries, the University of Southern Mississippi, the C. V. Starr Center for the Study of the American Experience at Washington College, Louisiana State University Special Collections, Firestone Library at Princeton University, Pascagoula Public Library Genealogy Department, Baltimore Museum of Art, Maryland Historical Society, the United Methodist Archives and History Center at Drew University, Amistad Research Center at Tulane University, the Schomburg Center for Research in Black Culture at the New York Public Library, Sankofa Special Collection at the Meadville Lombard Theological School, the Unitarian Universalist Congregation of Montclair, and the Historical New Orleans Collection. Montclair Public Library and Montclair History Center also provided helpful advice and connected me with useful resources.

Judy Riffel, Jan Hillegas, Renate Sanders, Shannon Brock, Ghita Johnson, and Patricia Watson researched and located information beyond my reach and shared it with generosity. Joel and Joan Brink, Peter Monrose, Francis Howcutt, Anne Andrews, Ginny Blair, and Ray Bellande shared vital information from their family archives and personal research. Sasha Condas and Morgan Loflin from Montclair High School Career Internship Program helped me stay organized.

Coming to the Table connected me with other people doing this difficult but sacred work, supported me in navigating enslavers in my family tree, and provided me with another home. I'm especially grateful to cofounder Susan Hutchison and members Shay Banks-Young and Dave Pettee who were so kind and inviting and who are all now with the ancestors.

Mrs. Bentzlin, my eighth-grade etymology and expository writing teacher at Frelinghuysen Junior School, encouraged me with notes like "you have an excellent imagination" in the margin of the journal she made us keep. Mentorship from Elizabeth Stone and Alice Elliott Dark helped me begin to see myself as a writer. Deborah Landau allowed me to work on this memoir at the NYU Creative Writing Program (even though I applied to work on a novel). My professors Zadie Smith and Joyce Carol Oates generously read and offered insightful feedback, and lent support to the book, as did Darin Strauss. I was transformed by my time at NYU and my classes with Zadie, Joyce, Hannah Tinti, Colson Whitehead, Nathan Englander, Susan Minot, and Anne Enright alongside an incredible cohort. Thank you Bsrat Mezghebe, Jessica Ramirez, Enkay Iguh, Jennifer Murphy, and Kathleen Furin for exchanging writing with me inside and outside of the classroom.

Karen Gerwin, Jackie Mroz, Deb Levy, Jill Hamburg Coplan, Nancy Williams, Ariel Zeitlin, Paula Derrow, Kara Richardson Whitely, Pari Berk, Addie Morfoot, Christina Baker Kline, Karen Branan, Rev. Scott Sammler-Michael, Cathy Chung, and Peter Hedges read everything from chapters to full drafts of this book and gave in-depth and helpful feedback.

The Unitarian Universalist Congregation of Montclair and the fellows around the world who practice the twelve steps are my spiritual home and family—thank you for always welcoming me. Carolyn Tricomi and Dawn Avery introduced me to many practical meditation tools that I still use today including the idea of personal altars, and Sharon Freedman and Cathy Roberts have helped me to expand my practice. My friends Patience Moore, Orlagh Cassidy, Jill Berke, Sharyn Mandell, Joanne Byrne, Carol Seymour, Vibe Clausen, and Deb Eiseman never allowed me to abandon this project or myself.

Friends now in the spiritual realm, whom I was lucky to know and love and who were always rooting for me: Erik Pedersen, Kevin Thomas, and Ellen Harnett. I miss you.

Finally, I thank my beautiful daughters, Desiree and Devany, and my husband, Dennis, for sustaining and loving me on this journey.

NOTES

PROLOGUE: A RELATION

1. See Steven J. Micheletti, Katarzyna Bryc, Samantha G. Ancona Esselmann, William A. Freyman, Meghan E. Moreno, G. David Poznik, Anjali J. Shastri, 23andMe Research Team, Sandra Beleza, and Joanna L. Mountain, "Genetic Consequences of the Transatlantic Slave Trade in the Americas," *American Journal of Human Genetics* 107, no. 2 (August 6, 2020), www.cell.com/ajhg /fulltext/S0002-9297(20)30200-7. To read more about the research, see Lizzie Wade, "Genetic Study Reveals Surprising Ancestry of Many Americans, *Science*, December 18, 2014, www .science.org/content/article/genetic-study-reveals-surprising -ancestry-many-americans; 23andMe, "An Analysis of the Ancestry Make-Up of People Across the United States," news release, December 18, 2014, https://blog.23andme.com/23andme-research /history-written-in-our-dna/; Christopher Ingraham, "A Lot of Southern Whites Are a Little Bit Black," *Washington Post*, December 22, 2014, www.washingtonpost.com/news/wonk/wp

/2014/12/22/a-lot-of-southern-whites-are-a-little-bit-black/; Jenée Desmond-Harris, "Here's Where 'White' Americans Have the Highest Percentage of African Ancestry," *Vox*, last modified February 20, 2015, www.vox.com/2014/12/22/7431391/guess-where-white-americans-have-the-most-african-ancestry; Carl Zimmer, "White? Black? A Murky Distinction Grows Still Murkier," *New York Times*, December 24, 2014, www.nytimes.com/2014/12/25/science/23andme-genetic-ethnicity-study.html; 23andMe, "23andMe Paper on Transatlantic Slave Trade Published," news release, July 23, 2020, https://blog.23andme.com/23andme-research/transatlantic-slave-trade-paper/.

2. "It is not wrong to go back for that which you have forgotten" is a translation of a proverb associated with sankofa, from the Twi language, "Se wo were fi na wosankofa a yenkyi."

CHAPTER 1: BLACK ON THE INSIDE

1. "We Wear the Mask" is the title of Paul Laurence Dunbar's poem, perhaps his most famous, which speaks to the double consciousness that Black Americans deploy in order to navigate in a racist world.

CHAPTER 2: BORROWING HISTORY

1. The attribution to Isabel Wilkerson comes from her talk "The Great Migration and the Power of a Single Decision," TEDWomen 2017, video, 17:46, www.ted.com/talks/isabel_wilkerson_the_great_migration_and_the_power_of_a_single_decision?language=en.

2. "For the cramped bewildered years" is a phrase from Margaret Walker's poem "For My People."

CHAPTER 3: BEATING BACK THE FUTURE

1. Henry Louis Gates Jr., "Exactly How 'Black' Is Black America?," The Root, February 11, 2013, www.theroot.com/exactly-how-black-is-black-america-1790895185.

2. "Incest," RAINN, www.rainn.org/articles/incest.

3. The American Psychological Association provides many facts on Black women survivors of sexual assault in Jameta Nicole Barlow, "Black Women, the Forgotten Survivors of Sexual Assault," *In the Public Interest*, February 2020, www.apa.org/pi /about/newsletter/2020/02/black-women-sexual-assault.

4. Hilda Hutcherson, "Black Women Are Hit Hardest by Fibroid Tumors," *New York Times*, April 15, 2020, www.nytimes .com/2020/04/15/parenting/fertility/black-women-uterine -fibroids.html.

5. Centers for Disease Control and Prevention, "Racial and Ethnic Disparities Continue in Pregnancy-Related Deaths," news release, September 5, 2019, www.cdc.gov/media/releases/2019 /p0905-racial-ethnic-disparities-pregnancy-deaths.html.

6. Precious Fondren, "One State's Approach to Maternal Deaths: Free Nurse Visits After Birth," *New York Times*, July 29, 2021, www.nytimes.com/2021/07/29/nyregion/maternal-mortality -new-jersey.html; "Combating New Jersey's Maternal and Infant Mortality Crisis," Nurture NJ, Office of Governor Phil Murphy, State of New Jersey, https://nj.gov/governor/admin/fl/nurture nj.shtml.

CHAPTER 4: EVERYTHING THE MOUTH EATS

1. See Tom Reiss, *The Black Count: Glory, Revolution, Betrayal, and the Real Count of Monte Cristo* (New York: Crown, 2012), for more information on Thomas-Alexandre Dumas and late-eighteenth-century French concepts of "American."

2. I first saw the picture of my great-great-grandparents on the website oceanspringsarchives.net.

3. Darlene Clark Hine, "Rape and the Inner Lives of Black Women in the Middle West," *Signs* 14, no. 4 (1989): 912–920, www.jstor.org/stable/3174692.

4. I learned about the study on the long-term effects of sexual abuse on female development and the *Comprehensive Textbook of Psychiatry* from Bessel van der Kolk, *The Body Keeps the Score: Brain,*

Mind, and Body in the Healing of Trauma (New York: Penguin, 2014), 190–191. Results of the twenty-five-year-long study that I cite can be found here: Penelope K. Trickett, Jennie G. Noll, Frank W. Putnam, "The Impact of Sexual Abuse on Female Development: Lessons from a Multigenerational, Longitudinal Research Study," *Development and Psychopathology* 23, no. 2 (May 2011), https://pubmed.ncbi.nlm.nih.gov/23786689/.

5. Dani Shapiro interviewed Bessel van Der Kolk on "Family Secrets Live: In Conversation with Dr. Bessel van der Kolk," May 7, 2020, in *Family Secrets*, podcast, www.iheart.com/podcast/105-family-secrets-30131253/episode/family-secrets-live-in-conversation-with-62203761/.

CHAPTER 5: PARADISE LOST

1. I found the information on the *Barque Pioneer* and the people it carried on Ancestry.com. "Slave Manifests of Coastwise Vessels Filed at New Orleans, Louisiana, 1807–1860," NARA microfilm publication, National Archives. The other information on the Colonel comes from an 1850 federal census and an 1850 slave schedule. The information on his sugar plantation comes from a January 1853 article that was forwarded to me.

2. The newspaper that reports on Tempy's death was "Oldest Person in Jackson County Dies," *Daily Herald*, March 10, 1925, p. 6.

3. William Makepeace Thackeray, quoted in Thomas Ruys Smith and Tom Hall, "Travelling to New Orleans, Now and in 1858," BBC Travel, July 5, 2011, www.bbc.com/travel/article/20110630-travelling-to-new-orleans-now-and-in-1858.

4. Virginia Meacham Gould, "Gender and Slave Labor in New Orleans," in *Discovering the Women in Slavery*, ed. Patricia Morton (Athens: University of Georgia Press, 1996), 192.

5. To understand what the domestic slave trade in New Orleans was like in the Colonel's day, I read this excellent article: Edward Ball, "Retracing Slavery's Trail of Tears," *Smithsonian*, November 2015, www.smithsonianmag.com/history/slavery-trail-of-tears-180956968/.

CHAPTER 6: PASSING STRANGE

1. The medical information on my aunt Shirley Ford comes from the East Louisiana State Mental Hospital records at the Louisiana State Archives.

2. Jill Lepore, "Obama, the Prequel," *New Yorker,* June 25, 2012, www.newyorker.com/magazine/2012/06/25/obama-the-prequel.

3. Toni Morrison, "Nobel Lecture," December 7, 1993, Nobel Prize, www.nobelprize.org/prizes/literature/1993/morrison/lecture/.

CHAPTER 7: UNITED DAUGHTERS

1. Silvana Siddali, *From Property to Person: Slavery and the Confiscation Acts, 1861–1862* (Baton Rouge: Louisiana State University Press, 2005), 52–54. I found this quote and citation in this excellent essay by Adam Rothman, "Nothing to Stay Here For," *Slate,* September 22, 2015, https://slate.com/human-interest/2015/09/the-end-of-slavery-in-new-orleans.html#:~:text=Union%20authorities%20clashed,the%20imagination.%E2%80%9D8.

2. Daina Ramey Berry and Kali Nicole Gross, *A Black Women's History of the United States* (Boston: Beacon Press, 2020), 97–98.

CHAPTER 8: THE PECAN AND HOW TO GROW IT

1. "Marriage of a Mexican Editor in Maryland," appeared in the *Baltimore Sun,* July 22, 1877. "Death of a Distinguished Southerner," appeared in *Daily Picayune,* April 1, 1894, 10.

CHAPTER 9: THE FIRE THIS TIME

1. For information on H. L. Stewart and the Switzers, I relied on Ray L. Bellande, "Doctors, Mayors & Aldermen," Ocean Springs Archives, https://oceanspringsarchives.net/doctors-mayors-aldermen; 1900 census; Ancestry.com for H. L. Stewart, Ocean Springs, MS; oceansprings.net, Ross Adams Switzer and Oren Switzer; and Regina Hines Ellison, *Ocean Springs, 1892* (self-published), 80.

2. See *Cutter's Guide to Mount Clemens*, n.d., Library of Congress, https://ia802705.us.archive.org/3/items/cuttersguidetomt00cutt /cuttersguidetomt00cutt.pdf; Dorothy M. Magee, ed., *The Centennial History of the Mount Clemens, Michigan, 1879–1979* (Mount Clemens, MI: Mount Clemens Public Library, 1980), ch. 5; Kimberly Parr's article on Henry Lightbourne in the Historical Society of Michigan's *Chronicle* Winter 2014 publication.

CHAPTER 10: SPIRITS

1. The letters between Carl Jung and Bill Wilson were published in the *AA Grapevine* in January 1963.

CHAPTER 11: HERETIC

1. The letters and information pertaining to William R. Stuart and his sons come from the William R. Stuart Papers, Manuscripts Division, Special Collections Department, Mississippi State University Libraries, https://msstate-archives.libraryhost.com /repositories/5/resources/59; and the Edward Lloyd Papers, archived at the Maryland Historical Society.

2. The UU Montclair history was accessed in the church's archive but can also be read in part here: "History," Unitarian Universalist Congregation at Montclair, www.uumontclair.org /history/.

3. The information on my great-grandfather James Ford is taken from Mississippi Annual Conference Methodist Episcopal catalogues archived at Drew University and several articles from the *Southwestern Christian Advocate*. The last quote in the chapter comes from *Southwestern Christian Advocate*, August 8, 1889, 1.

CHAPTER 12: GOOD AS COUSINS

1. Shaila K. Dewan and Ariel Hart, "Thurmond's Biracial Daughter Seeks to Join Confederacy Group," *New York Times*, July 2, 2004, www.nytimes.com/2004/07/02/us/thurmond-s-biracial -daughter-seeks-to-join-confederacy-group.html.

2. Saidiya Hartman, "Venus Is Two Acts," *Small Axe* 26 (June 2008): 11.

3. Nell Irvin Painter, "Soul Murder and Slavery" (Fifteenth Annual Charles Edmundson Historical Lectures, Baylor University, Waco, Texas, April 5–6, 1993), 9.

4. Attributed to Ida B. Wells.

CHAPTER 13: JUNETEENTH

1. Tempy Burton's Lost Friends ad and her response to the original query in the *Southwestern Christian Advocate* are archived at Historic New Orleans Collection/Hill Memorial Library, Louisiana State University Libraries, Baton Rouge, LA, and can be viewed here: www.hnoc.org/database/lost-friends/index.html.

2. See Harriet Jacobs [Linda Brent], *Incidents in the Life of a Slave Girl* (Boston, 1861), 77, https://docsouth.unc.edu/fpn /jacobs/jacobs.html.

3. The information about Henry Bibb comes from *The Narrative of the Life and Adventures of Henry Bibb, an American Slave, Written by Himself* (New York, 1849), 190 (archived at the University Library, University of North Carolina at Chapel Hill, Documenting the American South, https://docsouth.unc.edu/).

CHAPTER 14: PLANTATION DIARIES

1. Information on the Hilliard family comes from Ree Herring Hendrick, *Lineage and Tradition of the Herring, Conyers, Hendrick, Boddie, Perry, Crudup, Denson and Hilliard Families* (1916); "Nash County Slavery Petitions, North Carolina, 1818," NCGenWeb, Deloris Williams, researcher and submitter; and Timothy Wiley Rackly, *Nash County North Carolina, Division of Estate Slaves & Cohabitation Record, 1829–1861* (Kernersville, NC: T.W. Rackley, 1998), 1–2.

2. National Register of Historic Places, application for the Robert Carter Hilliard House; and Charles and Lucy Hilliard McVea Papers, Mss. 5159, Louisiana and Lower Mississippi Valley

collections, Louisiana State University Libraries, Baton Rouge, LA.

3. Information on the Stirling family comes from the Lewis Stirling and Family Papers, Mss. 1866, Louisiana and Lower Mississippi Valley Collections, Louisiana State University Libraries, Baton Rouge, LA, and research by Judy Riffel.

4. The passing reference is to "Ms. Lively and Mr. Sam, the first belonging to Stewart." Solomon Northup, *Twelve Years a Slave*, 167, Kindle.

5. The lineage of Primus's great-great-great-grandson Alton Sterling was determined through family member Osbern Sterling.

CHAPTER 15: TEMPY'S LOT

1. Ray L. Bellande, "Early Black Education," Ocean Springs Archives, https://oceanspringsarchives.net/early-black-education.

2. Details about Tempy's property, mortgage, and parcels she conveyed to Violet and Josephine comes from the Jackson County Assessment Rolls, Chancery Clerk, Pascagoula, Mississippi.

CHAPTER 16: A CROWD OF SORROWS

1. The articles on the lynching of my great-grand-uncle Warren were published in the *Daily Herald* (Mississippi), February 3, 1901; *Daily Item* (New Orleans) February 3, 1901; *Augusta Chronicle*, February 3, 1901; *Times Picayune*, February 4, 1901; *Trenton (NJ) Evening Times*, February 4, 1901; *Columbus Daily Enquirer*, February 3, 1901; *Idaho Statesman*, February 3, 1901; *Richmond Planet*, February 1901.

2. Asha DuMonthier, Chandra Childers, and Jessica Milli, *The Status of Black Women in the United States* (Washington, DC: Institute for Women's Policy Research, 2020), https://iwpr.org/iwpr-issues/race-ethnicity-gender-and-economy/the-status-of-black-women-in-the-united-states/.

3. Hazel V. Carby, *Reconstructing Womanhood: The Emergence of the Afro-American Woman Novelist* (Oxford: Oxford University Press, 1987), 39.

CHAPTER 17: MEETING THE STUARTS

1. The letters cited by William R. Stuart are from the Joseph Wickes Papers, archived at Washington College, Chestertown, MD, and from the William R. Stuart Papers, Manuscripts Division, Special Collections Department, Mississippi State University Libraries, https://msstate-archives.libraryhost.com/repositories/5/resources/59.

CHAPTER 18: COMING TO THE TABLE

1. The information on Alfred Stuart comes from Regina Hines Ellison, *Ocean Springs, 1892*, 49–50 and oceanspringsarchive.net.

2. Sylvia's quote comes from the booklet *Coming to the Table, A Collection of Stories: Coming to the Table Participants Share Some of What Their Family History Means to Them Today*, https://comingtothetable.org/wp-content/uploads/2019/08/CTTT-Collection-of-Stories.pdf.

3. Farmer-Paellmann directed me to this article as the source of the quote: "The Woman Who Took on Big Companies with Links to Slavery," *Descendants*, podcast, BBC Radio 4, www.bbc.co.uk/programmes/articles/1wRZx98QC3ry9DVk93H3JRG/the-woman-who-took-on-big-companies-with-links-to-slavery.

4. Woullard Lett's comment was made during a UU meeting on Zoom in April 2022.

CHAPTER 19: MONUMENTS

1. Equal Justice Initiative, *Lynching in America: Confronting the Legacy of Racial Terror*, 3rd ed. (Montgomery AL: Equal Justice Initiative, 2017), 27; Anne Moody, "The Movement," in *Coming of Age in Mississippi* (New York: Dell, 1968), 286, 338.

2. Van der Kolk, *The Body Keeps the Score*, 150.

EPILOGUE: ALTARS

1. Ted Andrews, *Animal Speak: Dictionary of Bird Totems* (Woodbury, MN: Llewellyn, 1993), 158.

2. The information on Allen Burton was found in *Digital Library on American Slavery's Race and Slavery Petitions Project*, Petition #20183903, abstract archived at the Schomburg Center for Research in Black Culture, New York Public Library, New York, NY.

3. John Newton's journal, June 24, 1754, can be accessed here: John Newton, "The Journal of a Slaver," Learning for Justice, www.learningforjustice.org/classroom-resources/texts/hard-history/the-journal-of-a-slave-trader.

BIBLIOGRAPHY

Achebe, Chinua. *Things Fall Apart.* New York: Ballantine, 1983.

Alcoholics Anonymous Big Book. New York: Alcoholics Anonymous World Service, 2007.

Barks, Coleman, trans. *The Soul of Rumi.* New York: Harper-Collins, 2001.

Berry, Daina Ramey, and Leslie M. Harris, eds. *Sexuality and Slavery: Reclaiming Intimate Histories in the Americas.* Athens: University of Georgia Press, 2018.

Brown, William Wells. *Clotel; or, the President's Daughter.* 1853.

Butler, Octavia. *Kindred.* Boston: Beacon Press, 1979.

Carby, Hazel V. *Reconstructing Womanhood: The Emergence of the Afro-American Woman Novelist.* Oxford: Oxford University Press, 1987.

Cone, James H. *God of the Oppressed.* Maryknoll, NY: Orbis Books, 1997.

Covington, Stephanie S. *A Woman's Way Through the Twelve Steps.* Center City, MN: Hazelden, 1994.

Dawsey, Cyrus B., and James M. Dawsey. *The Confederados: Old South Immigrants in Brazil.* Tuscaloosa: University of Alabama Press, 1995.

Dillard, Annie. "To Fashion a Text." In *Inventing the Truth: The Art and Craft of Memoir,* edited by William Zinsser. Boston: Mariner Books, 1998.

Dunbar, Paul Laurence. "We Wear the Mask." In *The Complete Poems of Paul Laurence Dunbar.* New York: Dodd, Mead and Company, 1913.

Everett, Percival. "The Appropriation of Cultures." In *Damned If I Do.* Minneapolis: Graywolf Press, 2004.

Gould, Virginia Meacham. "Gender and Slave Labor in New Orleans." In *Discovering the Women in Slavery,* edited by Patricia Morton. Athens: University of Georgia Press, 1996.

Gutman, Herbert G. *The Black Family in Slavery and Freedom 1750–1925.* New York: Vintage, 1976.

Harper, Frances Ellen Watkins. *Iola Leroy; Or, Shadows Uplifted.* Philadelphia: Garrigues Bros., 1893.

Hine, Darlene Clark. "Rape and the Inner Lives of Black Women in the Middle West: Preliminary Thoughts on the Culture of Dissemblance." *Signs* 14, no. 4 (1989).

Hurston, Zora Neale. *Mules and Men.* New York: HarperCollins, 1990.

———. *Their Eyes Were Watching God.* New York: Amistad, 2006.

Itapoan, Cesar. *The Saga of Mestre Bimba.* North Arlington, NJ: Capoeira Legados, 2006.

Ivker, Robert. *Sinus Survival: The Holistic Medical Treatment for Allergies, Colds and Sinusitis.* New York: Tarcher/Putnam, 1988.

Jacobs, Harriet [Linda Brent]. *Incidents in the Life of a Slave Girl.* Boston, 1861.

Lorde, Audre. "The Uses of Anger: Women Responding to Racism." In *Sister Outsider.* Berkeley: Crossing Press, 1984.

Lyerly, Cynthia Lynn. "Black Methodist Women in Slave Society." In *Discovering the Women in Slavery,* edited by Patricia Morton. Athens: University of Georgia Press, 1996.

Malcolm X and Alex Haley. *The Autobiography of Malcolm X.* New York: Ballantine Books, 1965.

Mason, Gilbert R., with James Patterson Smith. *Beaches, Blood, and Ballots: A Black Doctor's Civil Rights Struggle.* Jackson: University Press of Mississippi, 2000.

Miles, Tiya. *All That She Carried: The Journey of Ashley's Sack, a Black Family Keepsake.* New York: Random House, 2022.

Moody, Anne. *Coming of Age in Mississippi.* New York: Dell, 1968.

Morrison, Toni. "The Site of Memory." In *Inventing the Truth: The Art and Craft of Memoir,* edited by William Zinsser. Boston: Mariner Books, 1998.

———. *Song of Solomon.* New York: Knopf, 1977.

———. *Tar Baby.* New York: Penguin. 1983.

Murray, Pauli. *Proud Shoes: The True Story of an American Family.* Boston: Beacon Press, 1956.

———. *States' Laws on Race and Color.* Athens, GA: Women's Division of Christian Service, 1950.

Nelson, Alondra. *The Social Life of DNA: Race, Reparations, and Reconciliation After the Genome.* Boston: Beacon Press, 2016.

Northup, Solomon. *Twelve Years a Slave.* Kindle.

Painter, Nell Irvin. "Soul Murder and Slavery." The Fifteenth Annual Charles Edmundson Historical Lectures, Baylor University, Waco, Texas, April 5–6, 1993. https://archive.org/details/soulmurderslaver0000pain/page/30/mode/1up?view=theater.

Potter, Eliza. *A Hairdresser's Experience in High Life.* New York: Oxford University Press. 2009.

Reed, Christopher Robert. *All the World Is Here: The Black Presence at White City.* Bloomington: Indiana University Press, 2002.

Reiss, Tom. *The Black Count: Glory, Revolution, Betrayal, and the Real Count of Monte Cristo.* New York: Crown, 2012.

Simic, Charles. "Ax." In *Charles Simic: Selected Early Poems.* New York: George Braziller, 2000.

Somé, Malidoma Patrice. *The Healing Wisdom of Africa.* New York: Tarcher/Putnam, 1999.

Stevenson, Brenda. "What's Love Got to Do with It? Concubinage and Enslaved Women and Girls in the Antebellum South." In *Sexuality and Slavery: Reclaiming Intimate Histories in the Americas*, edited by Daina Ramey Berry and Leslie M. Harris. Athens: University of Georgia Press, 2018.

The Twelve Steps and Twelve Traditions. New York: Alcoholics Anonymous World Service, 1994.

Twelve Steps of Adult Children Steps Workbook. Signal Hill, CA: Adult Children of Alcoholics and Dysfunctional Families World Service Organization, 2008.

Van Der Kolk, Bessel. *The Body Keeps the Score: Brain, Mind, and Body in the Healing of Trauma*. New York: Penguin, 2014.

Walker, Alice. *The Color Purple*. New York: Harcourt, 1970.

———. *In Search of Our Mothers' Gardens*. New York: Houghton Mifflin, 1983.

Walker, Margaret. "For My People." In *For My People, the Yale Series of Younger Poets*. New Haven: Yale University Press, 1942.

Ward, Jesmyn. *The Fire This Time*. New York: Scribner, 2016.

Wells, Ida B. *A Red Record: Tabulated Statistics and Alleged Causes of Lynchings in the United States, 1892–1893–1894*. Chicago: Donohue & Henneberry, 1894.

White, Deborah Gray. *Ar'n't I a Woman?: Female Slaves in the Plantation South*. New York: W. W. Norton, 1999.

Whitman, Walt. *Franklin Evans or the Inebriate: A Tale of the Times*, edited by Christopher Castiglia and Glenn Hendler. Durham, NC: Duke University Press, 2007.

Wilkerson, Isabel. *The Warmth of Other Suns*. New York: Random House, 2010.

Williams, Delores S. *Sisters in the Wilderness: The Challenge of Womanist God-Talk*. Maryknoll, NY: Orbis Books, 1993.

Williams, Heather Andrea. *Help Me to Find My People: The African American Search for Family Lost in Slavery*. Chapel Hill: University of North Carolina Press, 2012.

Willis, W. Bruce. *The Little Adinkra Dictionary: A Handy Guide to Understanding the Language of Adinkra*. Washington, DC: Pyramid Complex, 2015.

Dionne Ford is an NEA creative writing fellow and the coeditor of the anthology *Slavery's Descendants: Shared Legacies of Race and Reconciliation* (Rutgers University Press). Her work has appeared in the *New York Times*, *Literary Hub*, *New Jersey Monthly Magazine*, the *Rumpus*, and *Ebony* and won awards from the National Association of Black Journalists and the Newswomen's Club of New York. She holds a BA from Fordham University and an MFA from New York University. She lives in New Jersey with her husband and daughters. Visit Dionneford.com.

Photo courtesy of the author.